What people are saying about D
Happily

"Upbeat yet realistic...a gold mine of practical information in a user-friendly format."

—ArmChairInterviews.com

"Commonsense and biblically grounded approach...I only wished that I had the book 20 years ago when after a painful divorce, I eventually found the courage to remarry...I will [recommend] it to anybody who brings up the subject of remarriage."

—Dave Garcia, Worship Director,
North Coast Church, Vista, California

"The four key strategies for marital unity are superb and practical."

—Paul and Pauline Hicks, retired pastors

"Timely...[not just] another book about divorce...The second half of the book is so practical and deals with the nuts-and-bolts issues staring newly remarried couples in the face."

—Dr. Dan Casey, Senior Pastor,
First Church of the Nazarene, Little Rock, Arkansas

"I read this book three times the week I bought it. It's already helped me with my husband's kids...My husband stayed up late one night and read the whole book. It's great for anyone trying to raise a stepfamily. I highly recommend it."

—Jaimie Fisher, reader

"Remarried couples and those individuals considering remarriage will find excellent counsel in this sensitively written text."

—FaithfulReader.com

Moving
Forward
After
Divorce

DAVID & LISA FRISBIE

HARVEST HOUSE PUBLISHERS

EUGENE, OREGON

All Scripture quotations are taken from the HOLY BIBLE, NEW INTERNATIONAL VERSION®. NIV®. Copyright©1973, 1978, 1984 by the International Bible Society. Used by permission of Zondervan. All rights reserved.

Cover by Koechel Peterson & Associates, Inc., Minneapolis, Minnesota

Cover photo © Thinkstock / Inmagine

MOVING FORWARD AFTER DIVORCE
Copyright © 2006 by David and Lisa Frisbie
Published by Harvest House Publishers
Eugene, Oregon 97402
www.harvesthousepublishers.com

Library of Congress Cataloging-in-Publication Data
Frisbie, David, 1955-
   Moving forward after divorce / David and Lisa Frisbie.
     p. cm.
   ISBN-13: 978-0-7369-1764-3 (pbk.)
   ISBN-10: 0-7369-1764-0 (pbk.)
   1. Divorced people—Religious life. 2. Divorce—Religious aspects—Christianity. I. Frisbie, Lisa, 1956- II. Title.
   BV4596.D58.F75 2006
   248.8'46—dc22
                                          2006001337

Printed in the United States of America

06 07 08 09 10 11 12 13 14 / VP-MS / 10 9 8 7 6 5 4 3 2 1

*To faith-filled people who believed in us
very early in our journey*

Acknowledgments

Writing is a lonely profession, though less so in our case because we write together as husband and wife. The two of us counsel, speak, teach, travel, and write together, side by side, as a personal choice and a professional commitment.

Even so, writing can be lonely. With speaking, the audience is often only a few feet away: You can see facial expressions, hear questions, and maybe even get an ovation if all goes well. There's feedback, participation, and sharing to help you along. None of those helpful processes occur in writing. You sit at a computer and type. No one claps or whistles or nods approvingly. No one raises her hand with a question.

Because writing can be so lonely, as writers we are personally and professionally grateful for the amazing people at Harvest House who partner with us in all that we do. Among these are three we'd like to mention by name.

Our editor, Paul Gossard, continually improves our work and helps it connect with our readers more effectively. Paul's work transcends editing to include friendship: We genuinely value his wise advice and supportive counsel.

Terry Glaspey has guided our projects from the very beginning. Among other gifts, Terry is a renaissance man—an accomplished author and speaker in his own right who invests his energy helping others to succeed in print. Many of us within the Harvest House family owe our first steps, and many steps since, to his gifted encouragement.

Carolyn McCready serves an executive role, yet somehow finds the time to not only meet authors, but serve them with gladness. We've learned to trust her marketing savvy, her eye for good writing, and her keen sense of good business practices.

In addition to these there are graphic artists, sales and marketing staff, and a large team of gifted people working together toward a common goal: helping authors find their purpose and fulfill their calling.

Our writing is better, our call is clearer, and our daily lives are more fulfilling because of the generous investment that Paul, Terry, Carolyn, and others at Harvest House have made in helping us fulfill our purpose and live our dream.

Contents

A Horizon of Hope

Divorce is a death and a dying. Divorce is a death without closure; the dying continues.

Divorce is the death of together, the seemingly permanent end of forever. Meant for a lifetime, a marriage once soaring upward with bright promise has crashed in the dark shadows. Nothing remains but the grieving.

Every morning of the twenty-first century, many of us rise to face a new day without a partner. Someone promised us, "I do," but then didn't. Someone bravely said, "I will"—but when the times got tough, they wouldn't. Now we are alone, feeling branded with a daily sense of failure that shows itself in all we do.

Is there hope for those of us who die again with each new morning? Is there any reason to rise, brew some coffee, and dare to dream?

If there is such a hope, these pages strive to point out the direction from which it might arrive. Like a compass needle, which may waver at first, the truths here will eventually swing toward our soul's true north—toward the One who loves us, even in the midst of all our confusion and suffering. Regardless of other forces, the compass is not disoriented; its needle points confidently toward hope.

The ideas here beckon our gaze away from the debris at our feet and out toward the far horizon. Though it is still dark right now and night reigns, even so, somewhere out there is the edge over which dawn will break and the brightness will rise. Someone out there loves us with a permanent and lasting love.

Dare we believe it? Is it safe to care again?

This book explores such questions, believing that darkness may happen, but Light will speak the final word.

What if there is a horizon toward which you may move—even if slowly—with the sure and certain knowledge that the sun also rises? We write with the silent prayer that as you run, walk, or even crawl forward, you will see the faint but steady glow of a dawn that is surely on its way.

Go ahead and buy some sunglasses.

The future may be brighter than you know.

PART ONE

*Finding Pathways to
Renewal and Hope*

CHAPTER ONE

From the Death of a Dream, New Beginnings

SEEKING BALANCE, FINDING PURPOSE— IN THE MIDST OF SUDDEN PAIN

Divorce is a horrible thing,
but worse is succumbing to the
paralysis that can follow in failing
to move ahead with God's plan
for the lives involved.
—Jim Tufford

Amanda left a brief note on the kitchen table.

"I'm leaving," it said. "I'll be back later for the rest of my things."

Darren found the note on a Friday evening when he got home from work. At first, he thought it might be a practical joke. Leaving? He knew Amanda had been moody and unhappy lately, but she'd been through times like that before.

Leaving? His brain couldn't quite process it. What did it mean? Was she taking some time away? Was she going home to her mother for a while? How long would she be gone? When was she coming back?

He poured himself some cereal, ate, and tried not to think about it. He carefully reviewed his last conversation with Amanda, on the phone earlier that day. She had sounded fairly normal, he thought.

He called her cell phone, leaving his number as a page.

When Saturday and Sunday passed with no return phone call or any other form of contact, Darren began to realize something was changing. Amanda had stormed out of the house before, angrily going for a drive for a few hours, but she had never been gone overnight without telling him where she was going.

Monday morning arrived, and Darren went off to work as usual. He kept his thoughts to himself, not telling any of his friends or co-workers about his wife's absence. He remembers thinking that sooner or later his wife would be coming back.

He was wrong.

On Thursday, when he arrived home from work, most of the furniture and other belongings in his house were missing. Amanda had apparently come home that day and carried away "her stuff"—which included basically every useful piece of furniture as well as the sound equipment and video gear.

Darren was angry—but also in shock. Why had she taken so many things that didn't belong to her? Where was she taking them? Who had helped her empty out his house? She couldn't have lifted the furniture by herself.

He had a lot of questions, but no answers. He called Amanda's cell phone again, leaving his number when she didn't pick up. He made his page an "urgent" message this time.

When she finally did call him back, it was nearly two weeks later.

"I'm divorcing you, if you haven't figured that out yet," she said sharply. "I just can't take it anymore, and I'm tired of trying."

This was the first time the word *divorce* had ever occurred in a conversation between them. With his emotions a mix of extreme shock and significant anger, Darren struggled to control his attitudes and his words.

"Can we talk about this?" he remembers asking his wife.

"There's nothing to talk about," was her retort.

That was her final answer.

Enduring Rejection and Loss

Thousands of times each week, the scene between Darren and Amanda is replayed, with slight variations, in houses and apartments across the country. More than 18,000 divorces take place in the U.S. every week of the year, most of them by common agreement after a period of discussion and negotiation.

Yet in many cases the divorce is set in motion by just one party, not both, and it begins with a process of departure and abandonment—someone leaves. Having promised to be together "forever" and stay "until death parts us," someone changes their mind. One day they are at home, and things seem mostly or entirely normal. The next day—they're gone, and they're not coming back.

Darren's emotional stress quickly became physical stress. His health deteriorated daily as the drama of Amanda's leaving began to play out. By the time the divorce papers arrived, he was in ill health. He had been abandoned by someone he loved.

The departure of a spouse is one of the deepest shocks we can receive—all the more if it's unexpected. Darren's mental and emotional anguish displayed themselves in a range of physical symptoms. These were not imaginary ailments—he was truly sick. His suffering was emotional—yet it went beyond thoughts and feelings, affecting his physical health.

> Even if the marriage relationship may
> have seemed troubled or tense, when a
> partner makes a sudden decision to leave us,
> our emotions can overwhelm us.

Divorce by abandonment is similar to death in its shock and trauma. With a lingering physical illness, such as a long struggle against cancer, our emotions have time to prepare for the eventual suffering that we'll experience. Although our pain will still be great, our physiological systems have had time to adjust, in advance, to the possibility of loss. In a sense, we are "ready" to process our grief—we have seen it coming in advance.

However, when a soldier is killed in combat, or when a close friend dies in a tragic car accident, there is no time to prepare ourselves. The phone rings, there is a knock at our door, and suddenly our world collapses around us in a heap.

Divorce by abandonment is similar. Even if the marriage relationship may have seemed troubled or tense, when a partner makes a sudden decision to leave us, our emotions can overwhelm us. We go through phases of shock, denial, and anger that are very similar to the emotional stages that accompany the grieving of a death. We may find ourselves literally unable to function—"locked up" mentally or emotionally, befuddled by even the simplest of choices or decisions. Simply put, our emotional systems are overloaded by the bombardment of a sudden, intense, and highly negative stimulus.

Abandonment taxes our emotional responses and strains our ability to deal with other natural sources of stress within our environment. The departure of a spouse may heighten or exaggerate our reaction to other types of stress we commonly experience, including health difficulties or financial worries.

Being abandoned hurts. The mere existence of the pain surprises us, as does its relentless intensity. We suffer—and there seems to be no relief for what we are enduring.

Meg's experience was similar to Darren's. She came home one afternoon to find a note on the kitchen table just like the one Darren found. "I'm leaving," the note from her husband said briefly. "We'll talk later."

Meg stared at the note for a while, not quite believing it.

"In my heart, I think I knew he was gone," she says today. "I think I already realized he wasn't coming back; I just couldn't think clearly. My emotions were too jumbled; it was like my brain couldn't function..."

By the time she received what she calls "the speech," she was starting to recover her clarity of thought—enough to realize she was angry.

"I love you," she remembers her husband saying when they finally talked. "But it just isn't working out for us to be together. I'll always love you—but I think it's best if I live somewhere else for a while."

Confused, afraid, angry, upset—Meg registered many emotions, but she knew enough to recognize absurdity when she heard it: "I love you" means "I'm leaving you"?

The disconnect echoed loudly inside her. "He basically said the exact same thing to our kids," she recalls with a loud sigh of resignation. "He told them he loved them but that he needed to go and live somewhere else for a while."

The ridiculousness of the claim didn't fool Meg's children either.

"If Daddy loves us, why is he leaving?" Meg's daughter asked her.

"If he really loved us, he wouldn't leave!" insisted her oldest son.

Lacking a useful or creative response, Meg just shook her head wearily and said nothing at all. Her son was right, in her opinion.

Internal Pain, External Symptoms

Meg decided to process her emotions by seeing a counselor, admitting that she was angry and needed therapy. Darren dealt with his emotions by keeping his thoughts and feelings bottled up inside—literally becoming sick as he did so. These are typical responses to abandonment.

Central to the issue of abandonment is a feeling of being rejected. As with other types of trauma, how we process our suffering is critical to our journey toward healing and recovery. While dealing with issues of rejection and abandonment, many people who never before considered seeing a counselor or psychologist make their first phone call for help. It's a call that, for many who experience divorce, begins to change their lives for good.

"Most of us experience rejection while we are young and dating," says Sharon, a family counselor on staff at a large church. "But when we get married, we believe our days of being rejected are over. After all, someone stands up in the front of the church and promises to love us forever!"

That is why, she explains, the pain of rejection is even greater when it comes from a partner we presumed would be lifelong and "forever."

While we are young someone may break up with us, dashing our heart into little pieces. Most of us learn to endure that type of pain. We gradually resume our search for a lasting love. We understand the temporary nature of teenage alliances—and we steel ourselves inwardly against the loss of affection or the end of the relationship. Even so, we continue hoping for something better—a union that lasts and endures.

Our deeper search—a quest for committed and permanent love—drives many of us toward a legal, even a religious expression of our unified life. We pledge ourselves to love one another within a marriage. We want a ceremony and a document that record our commitment to each other as binding and irreversible. We register for gifts, reserve a church, and invite friends and family. Consciously or unconsciously, we are striving to etch a permanent record of a love we assume will be lasting and durable.

Marriage, with its public, verbal expression of lifelong commitment to each other, appears to be a safe haven from the dark dangers of rejection. We make and receive strong assurances from our partner: In sickness and health, in prosperity and poverty, in good times and bad, our partner pledges to always be there for us. We make the same promise in return. All who attend hear us; everyone witnesses these profound vows. We celebrate.

Then, having found a place of seeming safety, we are even more surprised when someone hurts us. Our pain is greater because it comes from someone we love, trust, and value—someone who has received our trust and who is now deciding to break it. That someone may say, "I love you" on their way out the door—but we know better.

If they really loved us, they wouldn't leave us.

Darren's feelings of being rejected caused him to become ill; he remained so for several years after his wife left him. His slow return to physical health did not begin until he tentatively eased back into a normal social life, spending time with good friends and even starting to date again.

Although he could have sought counseling he did not, preferring to keep his feelings private. Only as time passed did he gradually return to his prior social patterns and friendships. Eventually, his physical symptoms eased. He began sleeping better at night and worrying less while awake.

"I think counseling might have saved me some time," he says today, "but I wasn't ready for it back then. I've always been the kind of person who keeps his thoughts and feelings to himself. Maybe I shouldn't be that way, but that's how I am. And when I'm hurting, that's even truer."

Meg's deep feelings of rejection impelled her to seek counseling quickly, a choice she readily recommends for others who have been abandoned.

"It took a while, but the counselor showed me that my husband's departure was basically his loss," she relates. "My counselor convinced me I was a healthy, likable, 'normal' person—not someone who deserved to be rejected and abandoned, not someone who had chased her partner away.

"Over time, and with my counselor's help, I began to see my husband's abandonment for what it was—a profound immaturity on his part, not the result of some deformity or defect in me. That took a while, but I can't tell you how much energy and health I felt once I realized my husband's abandonment of me—and our kids—said a lot about him, but nothing much about me. I'm not saying I'm perfect, but I was ready and willing to change, grow, and improve to help our marriage work."

Meg's counselor expresses similar thoughts: "The person who runs away is admitting their own immaturity and their own stubborn unwillingness to work things out. That speaks volumes about who they are, but guess what—it doesn't necessarily say anything about who they're leaving.

"We can safely assume no one is perfect—including the partner being left behind. Having said that, we can also safely assume that one partner, the departing one, is choosing the easy way out—instead of working on the problems and moving forward, the less mature partner is choosing to run away.

"Running away is immature. How many ways can we say that?" wonders Meg's counselor. "Abandoning your spouse is taking the easy way out."

As we process our internal pain and its external symptoms, we'll need to learn how to identify and respond to our feelings. Some of those feelings—and their intensity—may surprise us greatly.

Dealing with Guilt, Shame, and Social Stigma

In a nation that experiences a million divorces annually, it seems hard to accept the idea that significant social stigma still attaches to such a common occurrence. Yet in the minds of those who live through a divorce and its aftermath, there may be deep inner feelings of guilt, shame, and failure that transcend social mores and emerging trends. This is especially true within the religious community.

"Marriage is forever," Susan says simply. "When my marriage ended, so too did my sense of being a 'good' or 'acceptable' person within my church. Now I belonged to a whole new category—I was a divorced person. I felt like I had just been moved to a much lower social class. Maybe no one else felt that way when they thought about me, but that's exactly how I felt about myself."

Churches probably don't intend to send this message. Nevertheless, divorced persons may immediately feel as if they don't fit in anymore.

"My first Sunday as a divorced person, the pastor preached about the sanctity of marriage," Emily exclaims. "The very first Sunday! And it was a good sermon, but the only part I heard that day was 'God hates divorce.' There isn't anything else I remember from that message—just a high view of marriage and a complete rejection of divorce as an option for believers.

"Do I have to explain in detail how that made me feel? I'm sure no one, especially not the pastor, intended to insult me or offend me. I know that. But I also know how I felt—it's like everyone else around here measures up to the standard, but as a divorced person I was suddenly less than everyone else. Basically, I must not be a 'good' believer anymore, according to that sermon, because good believers know divorce is not okay. Good believers don't get divorces. I guess they somehow 'win' over every marriage problem!"

Feeling like a failure, the newly divorced woman quit attending her home church. It would be nearly two years before her next church service, this time in a place where no one knew her—and thus no one knew her personal history.

"When I did go back, I went to a singles service at a different church," Emily says softly. "And most of us in that group—once I got to know some people—were divorced like me."

The large and growing congregation featured an active ministry to divorced persons. In fact, the primary leader of the ministry was himself a divorced person, albeit one who had remarried. Together with his second wife, he led a community of several hundred single adults, many of them recently divorced.

"When I did dare to try a church again, I found one where divorced people are welcome, not judged," Emily explains. "I found a church, or maybe God led me to a church, where divorced people are just considered people—like everybody else. Nobody seemed to look down on me because I was divorced."

Whether or not churches, family groups, or social networks intend to attach a stigma to the aftermath of divorce, those who experience the end of a marriage often see themselves as outcasts, disappointments, or outright failures.

"My church is full of divorced people," Sandy says. "So when divorce happened to me, no one at church criticized me or seemed to look down on me. But privately in my own heart I felt like a complete failure.

"I would go to sleep at night—or rather, I would lie awake not sleeping—and I would think that somehow I had failed miserably at being married, that I would never have what it takes to be a good wife for someone.

"Those thoughts would just echo in my brain," she continues. "I hadn't heard them from anyone—not my parents, not my friends, not from people at church. But inside myself, there was this little voice constantly telling me I was a failure. I kept thinking: I had my chance, and now I've messed it all up."

Sandy's feelings are not unique. Many divorced people, and especially those who hold strong religious values, tend to regard divorce as outward evidence of an inner character flaw. It is assumed, and sometimes stated outright, that a person following God would never have ended up at a destination called divorce.

"Divorced" means "defective" in the internal self-talk of many religious persons. Whether or not this is openly taught in the congregation or the community, this is the core message that often forms in the minds and hearts of persons struggling through a divorce. And feeling defective and less than acceptable, divorced people are susceptible to feelings of guilt, shame, and failure.

When we sin against a known law of God, guilt and shame serve the useful purpose of calling us to repentance and forgiveness. As we reflect on our own lives and conduct, God's Holy Spirit searches our hearts, showing us places and situations where we may have been selfish or sinful. As with all instances of revealed sin, we need to confess our wrongdoing and then move in positive directions, turning away from evil. In such cases, our sense of guilt is positive—it impels us to examine our hearts, renounce our evil ways, and repent—turning away from wrong choices and negative directions.

Yet often our feelings of shame are not rooted in a willful act of rebellion against God or in a revealed sin. Instead, they may have their origin in the difficult circumstances of our lives, such as a divorce. We may carry a vague sense of personal failure about being divorced; we may internalize a sense of shame or inadequacy that is inappropriate and unhelpful. Looking around at those who seem successful and capable, we may feel "less than" or "unworthy of" others. If we had somehow functioned better as a husband or wife, we reason to ourselves, we would still be married. Others can do this better, we may feel, but somehow we are incapable of succeeding at it.

In such cases, our sense of guilt or shame may entrap us—limiting our ability to function in normal and natural ways. By seeing ourselves as unqualified or unworthy, we tend to fulfill our own low and negative expectations. We may underperform, underachieve, and spiral downward into depression or other physical or emotional afflictions.

Having Access to an Objective Listener

In such cases, we need to break free from the sense of shame or guilt that imprisons us in the miseries of the past. We are likely to need outside help as we confront our misconceptions about our own identity and our own future. A trained counselor or caring minister can be invaluable in the process of sorting through our feelings of shame. Without an objective listener, we may not make needed progress toward healing and recovery.

Cathy found it so. "I blamed myself for the divorce—not at first, but later, after the reality of things began to set in. At first I blamed my husband—he left me and moved in with another woman—but later I started blaming myself. I kept thinking that if I had been a more loving wife, or a more beautiful one, or if somehow I had taken better care of my husband—he would have never left me."

Cathy felt ashamed and inadequate about her performance as a wife and partner. She found herself constantly worried and anxious, thinking back on her five years of marriage, seeing herself as the person who had "caused" the divorce by failing, by falling short, by being less than perfect as a wife, mother, and household manager. Her sense of shame was partly about the fact of being divorced—yet at a deeper level it was rooted in low self-esteem, a nagging sense of self-doubt, and a lot of blaming herself for circumstances and situations beyond her control.

Six months into a regular weekly counseling regimen, Cathy began seeing things differently—especially herself. She began to accept herself as imperfect, as we all are, and yet realize that the primary responsibility for the end of her marriage had to rest with the person who decided to end it: her ex-husband.

"Gary wouldn't even consider getting counseling," she remembers. "Probably because he was already deeply into another relationship. I later found out he had been seeing this woman for the last year or so we were married.

"Looking back, I can't fully understand how I managed to blame myself for the fact that my husband was cheating on me, and that he left me. Now, when I look back, I can see that my sense of failure doesn't really make sense. But at the time, it was powerful. I had days when I thought I'd never succeed at anything again, and especially not at marriage or being a wife."

How did Cathy know she was beginning to heal? How did she become aware she was on the pathway toward recovery and balance?

Cathy's counselor helped her to process her feelings, learning to identify attitudes of self-loathing, self-doubt, and self-pity that inhibited healing. Along the way, as issues of personal development or personal growth emerged, these were noted by the counselor as places where she needed to make changes.

"I was blaming myself for too much of the problem," Cathy says today. "And yet at the same time, I didn't want to look too closely at some areas of my personal life, places where I really did need to change. I don't know how I did it, but I blamed myself unfairly, and also avoided having to grow up, at the very same time!"

How did Cathy know she was beginning to heal? How did she become aware she was on the pathway toward recovery and balance?

"I relaxed," she says simply. "In the weeks and months after my divorce, I was constantly tense. I became hypercritical of myself and also of my children. I would clench my teeth a lot, without knowing I was doing it. I had backaches, headaches, all kinds of symptoms—and didn't even realize that a lot of these things were due to the tension I was feeling. But after meeting with Carolyn [her counselor] for several months, I noticed I felt a lot more relaxed. I was sleeping better. I was nicer to my kids."

Could Cathy have achieved these same results on her own?

"Maybe. Maybe eventually I would have recovered. But Carolyn kind of 'got me going' in the healing process. She got me away from just treading water and feeling sorry for myself. She showed me how to start getting better instead of hating myself and blaming myself."

Fred's experience was similar. "I never thought I'd go to a counselor in my life." He shrugs. "But when Janet left me, I called my pastor and told him, 'We need to talk!' He dropped everything and made an appointment with me that same day. After that I started seeing him once a week, for two hours at a time. I talked and talked and talked—mostly venting all my anger and hostility—and I think Pastor Grant did nothing but listen for our first three or four sessions together.

"After that, once I had run out of angry words, Pastor helped me sort through my feelings and think clearly about myself and about Janet."

Does Fred recommend seeking pastoral care?

"Well, I would never have talked to Pastor Grant or anybody else, except I was hurting so bad," he admits. "If I hadn't been so angry, if I hadn't just had all the props kicked out from under me...I wouldn't have called him."

Nonetheless, Fred called his pastor and received genuine help.

"Pastor Grant helped me see things more clearly and accurately. He wouldn't let me drift off into blaming Janet or blaming myself. He just kept focusing on what my next steps should be."

For many who experience the trauma of being abandoned by a partner, one of the first steps toward recovery should be seeking the counsel of a wise and caring friend, a trained counselor, or a godly mentor or minister. Having access to an objective listener can mean the difference between stagnation and growth, between being stuck in the past and moving confidently toward the future.

"My feelings didn't make sense," is how Kaitlyn explains the aftermath of her sudden divorce. "I didn't know what I felt, I just knew I felt bad."

Kaitlyn's employer provided comprehensive health coverage, including a generous package of mental-health services. With only a per-visit deductible to pay, she was quick to enroll for counseling.

"I had low expectations," she acknowledges. "But I was so confused, I thought maybe a counselor could at least help me identify what I was feeling, could help me 'tag' my emotions and start naming them.

"What actually happened was that, after the first couple of weeks, I got a lot better at talking through my feelings. I would kind of realize what I was feeling once I started talking about it with my counselor."

Kaitlyn's experience is typical of those who are considered *verbal processors*. Verbal processors learn best by speaking: As they frame the words and ideas of a conversational exchange, they are literally realizing—in the moment—what their thoughts, attitudes, feelings, and opinions are.

In Kaitlyn's case, she discovered her primary issue was anger.

"I hated him!" she says of her ex-husband. "But before I saw the counselor, I couldn't have even told you that. As simple as that sounds—as basic—I hadn't even realized yet I hated my ex-husband. I'm trying to tell you this: I didn't even know what I felt, or how I felt, until I started going to those Friday-afternoon sessions."

Within the religious community, seeing a counselor may be viewed as a sign of weakness. After all, shouldn't "God alone" be sufficient?

We frame this question for Kaitlyn, who smiles ruefully.

"I really do believe God was helping me," she says forcefully, "but the way God chose to do it, was by using a counselor. It's like that story where God sends a rowboat and a helicopter to the people whose house is flooding. The people keep ignoring the boat and the other ways to escape because they insist God will rescue them.

"Later, after they drown and go to heaven, God tells them—'Hey, I sent you a boat and a helicopter!'—and they finally realize God was trying to rescue them all the time.

"In my case, it was God who rescued me—and I mean that literally—but the way He chose to do it was by using the counselor. My counselor was God's way of helping me get better."

Markers Along the Pathway

"I don't consider myself 'healed' from my divorce," says Sarah, five years after being divorced by Don. "I think it will always affect me. But I do know exactly when I realized I was getting better. Before that, I would lie down at night and be filled with all these bitter, angry, painful thoughts about the past, about being married, about being lied to.

"One night I was getting ready for bed, alone, and I realized I had been busy thinking about things I wanted to do over the weekend—errands to run, some places I wanted to go—and I just kind of realized all at once, maybe I'm starting to make some progress."

Had Sarah been seeing a counselor?

"Sort of." She laughs. "I was talking about everything with my younger sister. It was weird, because growing up I had been the one she came to with all of her dating stuff and relationship stuff. Now, all those years later, I was the one going to her for advice."

Her sister helped her think clearly and objectively about her situation, realizing what things were excess baggage—issues and feelings she shouldn't try to carry into the future.

"She didn't give me any free passes, either." Sarah can laugh about it now. "She was tough on me when she needed to be. But I also knew she loved me, and when I'd listen to her, I would know in my heart— what she was saying was true."

Today, Sarah is considering the possibility of getting remarried.

"There isn't anyone in my life right now," she insists. "But for the first time in a long time, I'm actually thinking I might not want to be alone for the rest of my life. I'm realizing I might want to share my life with a partner. Maybe God has someone out there for me, someone to share my life with."

It's an idea Sarah is talking about with her sister.

Regardless of her choice about remarrying, five years after her divorce Sarah is facing forward.

Coping with Abandonment:
How to Deal with Feelings of Rejection

Here are some key ideas to remember as you struggle with the feeling of being rejected or abandoned by a spouse:

1. *God will never leave you or forsake you.* Unlike what we experience in human relationships, God's love for us is permanent and unconditional. God has promised to love us and remain with us. "Nothing can separate us from God's love," Paul writes in the eighth chapter of Romans in the New Testament. Take time to reflect on God's character: God is faithful and true.

2. *Your children, parents, and friends are with you.* Your network may be small or large. Regardless of how many people you're close to, now is the time to reach out and stay connected with your children, parents, friends, and siblings. Remind yourself of the people in your life who care about you, who are committed to you, who will love you—for the long term.

3. *Rather than dwell in the past, turn and face forward.* There may be lessons to learn from your experiences. If so, learn them and move on. Don't allow yourself to spend hours, days, weeks, and months wallowing in despair, regret, or self-pity. Instead, focus on the possibilities and promises that are out in front of you. Face forward—look toward the future.

4. *Let others help you find your true strengths.* Talk with a pastor, a wise Christian believer, a counselor, or someone you trust. Ask them to help you sort through your attitudes and feelings in the midst of your pain. Ask them to help you identify, refine, and use your strengths in the days ahead; let them affirm how God has gifted you as a person, a parent, or both. Listen for the counsel of God in the voices of His people.

CHAPTER TWO

Embracing a Chance for Spiritual Renewal

DISCOVERING YOUR TRUE IDENTITY AS A CHILD OF GOD

*We are pregnant with possibilities
of spiritual growth and moral beauty
so great that they cannot be adequately described
as anything less than the formation
of Christ in our very lives.*
—John Ortberg

Judy got married because she wanted to escape from her home. Her father, an angry alcoholic, deserted the family when she was only four years old. Subsequently, her mother remarried—twice. Both of Judy's stepfathers were angry and uncaring, just as her birth father had been.

Both men were alcoholics, again an echo of her birth father's identity and values.

By the time she was 19, all three of her mother's marriages had ended—all three terminating in bitterness and anger. Her mother was living with a much younger man; to the best of Judy's knowledge, she did not intend to marry him. True to the pattern, however, the man was an alcoholic.

Judy, who was then attending a community college, began dating a friend from high school. When he proposed marriage during the Christmas holidays, Judy said yes immediately. "Anything had to be better than staying at home," is how she saw it. Although watching three marriages fail might have increased her caution, instead the failed marriages propelled Judy out of her birth family—and into a failed marriage of her own.

"I should have known better," she laments. "I, of all people, should have known to take it slowly and choose more carefully. But frankly, all I could see was a guy who loved me, who was fun to be around, and who was offering me a free ticket out of my house—away from my mom and her drunken men.

"You'd think I would have just moved out and lived on my own," she says today, with the wisdom of hindsight. "But it was the marriage proposal that became my way of escape."

Judy's marriage lasted nearly two years; yet for the final eight months or so of the marriage, Judy and her husband, Jim, were living apart, not together. By then it was obvious the marriage was headed for divorce.

"We were together about a year, and we were happy for maybe the first two months," Judy remembers. "We had about two good months together before we started fighting all the time. And the worst of it was—Jim was a drinker!"

Divorced before she turned 22, Judy was angry at herself for rushing into a quick marriage—and even angrier she had married an alcoholic. "I couldn't believe that after watching my mom get married to three drunks in a row, I went and did the exact same thing!" She shakes her head in disbelief.

Today, nearing 40, Judy is five years into her second marriage, a relationship that breaks the unhealthy patterns of her unhappy past. She and Jason are active members of a large congregation; they are involved in ministry to remarried couples and blended families.

Yet for a dozen years after divorcing her first husband, Judy chose to remain single. During that time, she made the long, slow journey from the anger and pain of her childhood into a gradual awareness of her own possibilities. Through counseling, and by learning to know herself better, she became a much better judge of character and potential in other persons as well as in herself. And as she chooses to explain the process, she had a lot of divine help.

Discovering How God Sees Us

"I sometimes think the only good thing about my first marriage is that we didn't have any children," Judy says today. "I was taking the pill, and thank God it worked for us."

Suddenly single again and still only 21 years old, she was faced with a brand-new start in life. She knew only one thing for certain—it was time to change the pattern set by her mother; it was time to learn how to live in healthier ways.

"I didn't change all at once," she recalls. "And really, for the last year of my marriage and the first few years of my divorce, I was mostly just resentful and angry. I didn't hate *Jim*—I hated myself for marrying him."

Judy began seeing a counselor before the divorce was final, and she continued with therapy for nearly three years. Even though at times she didn't think she could afford it, she viewed counseling as her only available lifeline.

"Those weekly sessions were my survival—absolutely," she explains. "Without a voice of sanity talking to me every week, I'm not sure where I would be today. I hated my mom; I hated myself. I thought I had managed to screw up my life beyond all help."

She got her counseling at a church-based clinic, yet she didn't attend the host church at any time during her therapy.

"No," she says with a wry smile, "I wasn't buying into that whole religious thing at the time. To be honest with you, my choice of a church-based counselor was really about the price. I looked at several options for counselors, and I decided I would choose the cheapest one—which was probably not the best way to choose!" She grins. "So every week I was going to a church campus and walking around where there were crosses and religious symbols everywhere, but I didn't even have curiosity about all that. If there was a God, I was sure He was mad at me for the choices I had already made. I didn't need one more angry father figure in my life. I was trying to erase the memories of all of that!"

Judy's counselor was an older man, who because of his age and gender might have embodied her unfortunate prior experiences with men. Instead, he became a gentle, calm, reassuring presence as she sought to understand the patterns of her unhappy childhood and married life.

"Week after week, I just sat there and poured my heart out," she recounts. "I felt like I could say anything in there—and I did! I just bubbled up with bitter, angry, hostile energy. I don't know how he put up with me..."

By the time Judy chose to end the counseling, she was beginning to feel relief from the bitterness of her past. She was beginning to realize that her future was not limited by the experiences of her childhood or her marriage. She was on the road to becoming a more confident, more positive, more optimistic person. Yet these positive outcomes didn't sufficiently motivate her to pursue spiritual or personal renewal. Having processed the major issues that confronted her after the divorce, she found her life simpler but still static.

Still Afraid

"Several years after I quit going to counseling, I still hadn't started dating at all," she recalls. "I was afraid of making a bad choice, so it seemed easier to not make any choices at all. I stayed busy with work. I kept away from any men that seemed interested in me."

Then Judy's pathway was intersected by a church-planned event. A postcard about a divorce-recovery program arrived in her mailbox.

"I couldn't throw it away," she marvels. "I took a magnet and stuck that postcard on the door of my fridge, where I kept seeing it."

All Judy heard was that God loved her. And hearing that message began to literally change her life.

As the date got closer, she couldn't get the event out of her mind. Finally, anxious and uncertain, she called the church office and reserved a seat at the Saturday-afternoon program. She told herself she didn't have to show up just because she had made the appointment. After all, people do change their minds.

Yet when the day arrived, she chose to show up.

"Being there that day changed my life," she says with a sigh. "For the first time in my life, someone told me that God loved divorced people. I mean, as simple as that sounds—no one had ever told me that! And it was the last thing I expected to hear from God—that He loved me. I assumed God had me on His 'bad list' or something—as a divorced person, I assumed I was some kind of a 'problem child' in His eyes."

Although the seminar included concrete, positive information about healing and recovery after divorce, all Judy heard was that God loved her. And hearing that message began to literally change her life.

Two weeks after the seminar, she made her way back to the church for a Saturday-evening service. "People were dressed very casually," she remembers. "I felt very comfortable, not threatened or judged or unwelcome. In fact, people didn't even seem to notice me—and I mean that in a good way. I didn't feel conspicuous or anything, as a newcomer."

The service included lively music, an inspiring time of teaching, and lots of complimentary coffee and cookies. Every ingredient in the mix was a complete surprise to Judy, a lifelong nonattender of church. Among her surprises was the wide mix of age and marital status among those attending the service. Yet mostly, Judy discerned a message.

"The music was great!" she exclaims. "And the teaching was full of useful information. It showed me God's heart, for one thing. God wasn't this mean-spirited, angry, judgmental figure anymore. God was kind and loving. God wanted the best for me. God wanted my life to work out for good."

A Point of Decision

After several months of irregular attendance, Judy came to what she terms a "point of decision" about her life.

"Our pastor talks about 'giving Jesus the steering wheel of your life' and 'crossing over the line' to become a Christian. And one Saturday after the service, I decided to make that choice then and there."

She stayed after the service and prayed with a staff minister. "It was quick and simple," she explains. "For me at least, it wasn't this big emotional event. I didn't cry. I didn't feel 'completely different.' For me, it just seemed like something I needed to do. I needed to let God into my life; I needed to quit trying to control everything and just let God work in my heart."

It was the beginning of a whole new beginning.

"Everything changed," she says with fervor. "Although I didn't particularly feel it or even notice it, everything changed from that moment on."

Several weeks later, reading her Bible and learning how to pray, Judy realized that the stress and tension in her life was remarkably lessened. She began to relax and accept herself. Surprisingly, at least to her, she began to enjoy her job and relate more positively to people at work.

"One of my girlfriends at work was the first to say something. She came up one day and said, 'You seem more relaxed than usual,' or words to that effect. So I was able to tell her, very matter-of-factly, that I had asked God to be more involved in my life."

Was this decision somehow explained or encouraged at the original divorce seminar that Judy had attended? Had it dealt with religious experiences or spiritual transformations?

"Oh, no," she says. "That day was just about healing from divorce. Nobody was pushing any religious agenda that day—I would have noticed. But we did hear that God loved us. It was hearing that message that began my change of heart. Hearing that message opened me up to the possibility of coming around a church and its ministries. Hearing that message convinced me God was not my sworn enemy—maybe He was a long-lost friend."

Less than two years after "giving Jesus the steering wheel of her life," Judy was featured as a speaker at a Saturday-afternoon divorce seminar at the church and briefly told her personal story, including her conversion experience.

"I wasn't the main speaker, of course. But the people who were running the divorce-recovery program asked if I would talk about my own journey a little bit during the seminar, so I did. When the session was over, I had people coming up to ask me questions and find out more," she recalls. "I didn't feel like I had any answers—but it was easy and natural to just tell my own story. So I did."

Today, nearly five years into a fulfilling second marriage, Judy often tells her story at divorce-recovery seminars. She finds it liberating; her prayer is that other divorced men and women will find their way to God, as she did. "This church isn't about religion or politics at all," she comments. "This church is about people finding peace with God, and peace with themselves. It has literally changed my life. So for me, it's easy to tell people what I've seen here."

Receiving Peace from a Loving God

Judy's experience is far from unique.

"I wouldn't have survived this except for finding God," is how Janelle speaks about her divorce and subsequent spiritual journey. "My parents were dead, my children were young, and my husband walked out the door—I had no one. I threw myself into the religion of my childhood and found out there was actually something real there. When I went back to church after being away for a long time, I was surprised to discover a God who was real and personal and who loved me."

Janelle is unable to explain what drew her back to church.

"I just knew I was alone. I knew I didn't have the answers to what was happening to me, or what to do next. As I thought about my life, the idea of going back to church just sort of came to me."

Was this God at work, reaching out to Janelle?

"I don't know," she says. "At that point in my life, I wasn't religious or spiritual or anything else. I was confused. I was angry. I was clueless. I wanted someone to explain things to me. I wanted everything to make sense somehow."

Finding Friends

Is this what she found at church when she returned to it?

"Well no, not exactly," she relates. "What I found at first was a group of people who took an interest in me. They didn't seem to be judging me or looking down at me. In fact, of the first four or five women that I met and got to know at the church, two of them were divorced!" Janelle is amazed by this. "Who knew there were so many divorced people in the church? I mean, I never expected that."

She tells us something from her childhood. "I grew up in a very friendly church. I mean, I don't really know why I quit going there, except I was making some choices that probably weren't very 'churchy' or religious. I was sexually active as a teenager, and maybe I kind of knew God disapproved of that." She wrinkles her face. "Maybe I quit going to church because I didn't want someone to preach at me about morality and sex."

Years later, she was looking for answers about morality. "Yes," she admits candidly, "I probably knew, even as a teen, that I was making choices that were wrong, doing things that were harmful to me and others. But I was so busy living my life on my terms, I didn't want to listen to any of that. When my marriage crashed, it just seemed logical to go back to church and see if anyone had any answers.

"I went on a Sunday morning. And by later that same week, two different people had called to thank me for coming. They didn't try to sell me anything—they just told me they were glad I came. At that time of my life, confused and hurting, I didn't think I had two real friends in all the world," she says softly. "So for two strangers to call in the same week, just to be kind—it was hard to resist that much caring."

Janelle returned to the church the following Sunday, then established a pattern of attending almost every week, caught up in the caring of these new friends.

"I met one woman—she was divorced like I was," she explains. "She started calling and inviting me to coffee. I was a little bit standoffish at first; I didn't understand her motives."

After two or three invitations, Janelle said yes—and thus began what has become a deep and lasting friendship.

"Stacy is my best friend in the world," she says today. "She's been with me through this whole long process of trying to heal and start over. She's been so good for me—because she's gone through the same exact things. Her husband walked out on her, just like mine did. She had young children at home when that happened—so did I. So we had a lot in common right from the start, except that she knew God and I was clueless."

Yet Janelle changed in both respects.

"My life started changing in a small group," she says very quietly. "We were doing a Bible study based on the sermon from the previous Sunday. Some of the weeks were really interesting; some weeks were kind of boring. But what began to happen is that we got close to each other in that group. We were all single; about half of us were single after a divorce. We were all about the same age, or at least most of us were."

Making It Personal

"One week the sermon was very personal—it was about receiving God's forgiveness and welcoming God's presence in our life. I had to admit to myself I had never done that. I had never asked God to forgive me. I had never invited God to be active in my life or my choices. I was going to church all the time, and I was going to small group all the time—but nothing had become 'personal' yet. I was doing a lot of things right, but inside I was still hurting and afraid."

For Janelle, an evening at small group became a life-changing experience and the beginning of a whole new journey.

"Things finally made sense. I could see what was missing in my life. I could see what I needed to do about that. And doing that seemed like the most natural thing in the world."

Loved and Wanted

After praying, confessing, and asking God to forgive her, Janelle was surprised when the whole group gathered around her after her own prayer and began praying for her—out loud.

"It shocked me, to be honest." She smiles. "I hadn't seen that before—or maybe I had as a child, but I didn't remember it. So when people started praying for me, out loud, asking God to bless me—it was weird at first.

"Then, as I listened to the prayers—it just blew me away. All of a sudden I realized I had found a new family—a new family of people, but also a new family in God. I was God's child again—or maybe still. I wasn't some wandering person who was lost or confused. I was back in God's family, loved and wanted."

It was a process of coming full circle from her childhood experiences, yet it was also new and different to her. "I had never internalized my faith as a child. I had never come to the moment of asking God's forgiveness and then receiving it. So everything about the moment was new. I was crying, and I was feeling very loved—all at the same time."

Janelle was encountering God's presence and sufficiency. She was finding peace with a God who loved her. In a very real sense, she was coming home.

"Only now, years and years after my childhood Sunday-school classes," she explains, "do I really understand those lessons. Way back then, I had teachers trying to tell me God loved me. But I filtered all that through my childhood mind—God loved me when I did good; God hated me when I did bad. Nobody taught me that, but that's what I learned somehow.

"Only now, as an adult, coming home to faith for the first time, do I finally realize God has always loved me—when I chose bad, when I chose good. God was loving me the whole time I was staying away from

Him and His church. God was loving me when I married so unwisely, and God was loving me when that foolish marriage finally fell apart."

She echoes the question many divorced people raise: "Why did it take me my whole life to figure this out?"

Finding God to Be a Committed Partner

Before getting remarried, Gerald spent ten years as a divorced single father, raising two daughters and a son. His ex-wife, who might have otherwise seemed like a logical choice to be the custodial parent, was addicted to alcohol and an active user of "party drugs." The courts affirmed and upheld him as the more reliable choice for his children.

Religion, though, in any form or fashion, was not a part of his life. "I grew up in church and walked away as a teen," he confesses. "At some point I lost interest in whatever they were selling, or trying to sell me."

Although he had a church wedding, it was the first and only time he attended church as an adult—until he found himself divorced and the father of three young children. "I needed help," he says. "Not for me, but with the kids. Frankly, I was hoping the church could 'be there' for them in ways that I, as a single parent, just wasn't able to manage."

Selfish Motives

"Maybe it's unfair or something, but my motives in going back to church were completely selfish. I wanted to find programs or groups or camps or anything that would help my kids. I also hoped I would find adults that could show my kids what a 'normal family' was supposed to look like—since their own home was shattered, and their mom was a drug-addicted wreck."

Gerald attended three churches before finding what he thought he wanted: "We walked in, all four of us, and immediately hit a table full of donuts," he comments with a boyish grin. "Donuts! There were cookies too, I think, but my kids and I went right to the donuts. My son immediately said 'I like this church, Dad!' and I think it was all over," he laughs as he relates this part of the story.

Of course, a single parent does not live by treats alone. "The woman who took my youngest daughter off to child care," Gerald remembers, "had the warmest, most sincere smile I've ever seen on a person. She automatically seemed like someone I would trust. Maribeth seemed to like her, and as I watched the two of them head to the child-care room, I just knew in my heart that we had found a good church."

Not that he was seeking a religious experience of any sort. "Not for me, no," he insists. "And I didn't particularly want any kind of religious indoctrination for the kids, either. I just wanted them to learn some good values and be around some good people. I thought church was as good a place as any, to look for those things…"

"Partnering with God"

God apparently had other plans.

"I was invited to a men's retreat right away," Gerald reports. "And of course as a single father, I couldn't go. But it impressed me that people were trying to reach out and include me in things. I appreciated that—it didn't offend me, it 'befriended' me—in a good way."

When a Saturday-morning event for men happened a few months later, he decided to attend. "My parents would take the kids sometimes on a Saturday or Sunday—just to give me some time to relax, clean the house, or whatever. That Saturday my folks had the kids, and there was a men's event at the church that featured a major pro athlete and some other guys talking about how faith had intersected their lives.

> "I think I was having a 'divine appointment' and I just didn't realize it yet."

"I figured it couldn't be too 'preachy' since these were sports guys," he continues. "And I had always admired the athlete who was the main attraction. I kind of thought—*Why not go? What's the harm?*"

Gerald attended, meeting new friends and connecting with men he'd seen at the church but not interacted with. The atmosphere at the Saturday breakfast event was casual—the conversation humorous, the laughter constant.

Then the speaker started talking about God.

"His whole speech that day was about partnering with God," Gerald recalls, "but that wasn't the first thing I noticed. The first thing was, this guy was divorced and remarried. And he talked a lot about his divorce, probably more about that than the sports stuff. He wasn't bitter, he didn't seem angry. But he expressed a lot of the same things I'd been feeling since getting divorced. I think I was having a 'divine appointment' and I just didn't realize it yet."

When the speaker came to a part of his talk where he invited men to receive Christ into their lives and "partner with God" for the future, Gerald knew he needed to do so: "I was surprised I hadn't seen it coming! But by the time he got to that part of the speech, I knew in my heart that this was exactly what I needed.

"I didn't talk to anybody, including the speaker," he says. "I didn't fill out any cards or put my name on any lists. I'm not really a joiner. But in my heart, privately with God, I did invite Him into my life. I couldn't explain it, but I knew I was changing my life and giving God some kind of central role in helping me as a person and especially as a dad."

Did things change for him after that moment?

"You mean, did I get smarter all of a sudden?" Gerald laughs. "Not really. But I did feel like this huge weight was lifted off my shoulders. Although my parents had been helpful and some other friends had been there for me, I had been feeling like, if my kids were going to make it and turn out okay, it was all up to me. After that meeting, I felt lighter.

It was like I wasn't carrying around that whole big weight of being dad, mom, and everything else for my kids. I really did have a sense that God—wherever and whoever He was—had just signed on to help me raise my children."

No Longer Alone

Looking back, Gerald believes the process is working.

"Oh, man…I don't know how I could have survived any of those years without God as a partner and a helper. And now, even though I'm married to a wonderful woman, both of us still know we need God as a partner."

Can Gerald describe what partnering with God is like? Can he put it in practical terms others can understand?

"Well, like I said already, I felt 'lighter' right away," he begins. "That meant a lot to me, because I knew I wasn't making it up. I had a very tangible, very real sense I wasn't alone anymore. God was with me.

"Beyond that, I started learning how to pray. That was hard for me; I hadn't grown up in a home where anybody prayed about anything. I didn't know how to pray. But I started learning to pray and sort of ask God to help me, ask God for advice. And a day or two later, or a week or two later, sometimes I would have a real clear sense of what I should be doing. That didn't happen every time. That didn't happen on some kind of a regular schedule. But it was still real. It was absolutely, truly happening to me. I was asking God for wisdom, and God was answering my prayers and giving me a sense of what to do."

We ask for an example.

"Well, getting remarried is definitely the big one," Gerald sighs. "My kids liked Melissa a lot, we all did. I mean—I was in love with her. But getting married? I wasn't sure that was the answer. My first marriage ended badly—frankly, it was pretty bad all the way through. I wasn't sure I was ready to try again, especially if everything was going to fall apart again.

"So I was talking to some guys at church, and my parents, but then I started seriously praying about that, asking God if I should get remarried. Does this sound crazy? I know a lot of people think God doesn't get involved in the 'personal stuff' or the daily details. But I was praying about it, asking God if I should get remarried."

A Second Partner

Gerald continued praying this way for about four months. "The more I prayed, the more peace I had," he insists. "I would pray and do my best to listen for any sense of God's direction or instruction, and what would come over me is a sense of peace and calmness about getting remarried.

"I think that was God. Here's why—the peace I felt came because I was praying, when I was praying, after I had prayed. I was asking God for wisdom, and that's what I was getting. I was getting a sense of peace about remarrying, and that's what I needed, because I was afraid of it. Did God say, 'Get married to Melissa' in a loud voice? No. I didn't experience anything remotely like that. But I prayed—a lot—and every time I asked God to show me if I should get married to Melissa, I would be flooded with a sense of calmness and peace."

Gerald speaks with firm conviction and a clear voice. "Maybe other people can't connect with that," he says slowly. "But this whole thing has been absolutely real to me. And there have been a lot of other things I've taken to prayer, and I've just sensed God guiding and leading me to know what I should do."

Does Gerald consider himself a "changed" person?

He thinks for a while before answering the question. "Yes, in two ways," he says finally. "First and most important, I'm a changed person because God is in my life. God is guiding my life. Second—

maybe this isn't what you were asking—but I'm a changed person because I'm married to Melissa. She grew up with everything I didn't have: parents who walked with God and showed her what that looked like.

"I've learned so much about God from Melissa," he goes on to tell us. "She has shown me what it looks like, on a daily basis, to partner with God in this thing called life. Melissa has a kind of 'steady faith' that, no matter what happens, every morning when she wakes up God is going to be right there beside her, ready to help and guide and show her what to do.

"She doesn't just talk about that, she lives it. It's real in her, and every day it's becoming a little more real in me too."

Gerald concludes but then adds a final thought.

"I have two partners," he says. "God is the main one, but God has chosen to bring me another one. I am more grateful for that than I can possibly tell you..."

Butterfly Glimpses

When a worm becomes a butterfly it wraps itself in a cocoon, emerging later in a form completely different from what it was before: Now it has wings, it can fly. In between these two stages the worm's life involves darkness and change, the trauma and the struggle of transformation.

Somehow it is the dark seasons of life, the traumatic changes we are forced to endure, that often bring us the greatest possibility of being transformed into something new and capable: a butterfly with wings. Before, content with our self-reliant ways, we crawl forward on our bellies, inching along toward our own version of the future. Only later, after the trauma, do we realize we've been given wings to fly—we can soar to places we've only imagined.

Divorce is like that. Divorce shatters our old way of proceeding. It ends our comfortable life, or at least the life we had adjusted to as normative, forcing us to confront dark and frightening places. Yet it is in these very places that, as we rely on God and His wisdom, we can make real our transformation into new creations through Christ.

John Ortberg refers to this process as "morphing." In his wonderful writings about spiritual renewal and personal growth, he challenges us to be open to the transforming graces that characterize God's interactions with us. Only when we are caught in the grip of something greater than ourselves can we fulfill the high calling and brilliant design of our Creator.

In our weakest moments, in our lowest places, we can embrace a God whose love for us incorporates the seeming disasters of our lives and fashions them into beautiful new possibilities. As we allow God to lead us and direct our paths, we can expect to discover capabilities and capacities we've never known.

Kent, divorced after nearly eight years of difficult marriage, found himself spiraling downward into sadness and confusion. He had nothing but his faith to cling to, and on some days his faith felt futile at best. If there was a God, why had He allowed so much suffering to invade Kent's life and marriage?

"I didn't know what God was doing, but whatever it was, I reached the point where I just said, 'God, I'm all yours' to mold and shape and change," Kent recalls. "I didn't say that with high expectations. I said it more like a final prayer."

What Kent didn't realize was this: God was forming a leader to serve Him.

Today, active in ministry to divorced people, single parents, and remarried couples with blended families, Kent shakes his head in wonder at what God did. "I can't believe I'm in ministry!" There is awe in his voice.

"I can't believe God used the end of my marriage, and the terrible pain I felt, to change my direction in life and bring me into ministry as a vocation. It dazzles me," he says, looking off toward a far window. "I would not have imagined this life in a million years..."

By his own description, Kent is neither rich nor famous, neither "important" nor even "talented." Instead, he suggests another term we might use to describe him now. "I am...fulfilled," he says gently. "As I work with blended families, helping people figure out how to merge his kids, her kids, everyone's diverse expectations, and lots of bad memories into a somehow-happy new household, every day I marvel that God picked me up, dusted me off, and shaped me into a minister."

He is silent, contemplating this. "It's amazing to me. Not that I'm such a big helpful presence in people's lives, I'm not saying that. It's just that almost every day I am involved in helping people make life-changing adjustments to their marriage and their way of raising their children. Almost every day someone asks me for godly advice—me!—and I share with them what I've learned through all this."

He shakes his head. "I'll tell you this," he adds. "If God can take a guy with eight years of a bad marriage, then several years of depression and sorrow, and mold that guy into an optimistic, positive-thinking minister..." He lets the sentence remain unfinished for a moment.

"What I tell people is—anything is possible," he goes on. "Anything. There is no limit to what God might want to do with us. He may have a complete change of career or calling in mind for us. He may be about to open doors we could never have opened for ourselves."

In other words, when God gets involved—worms can fly. They

emerge from the darkness, soaring into the heights, their bright colors highlighted against the brilliant blue overhead. From the silent places and the hidden struggles, they emerge with wings.

If the pain and damage of your past have trapped you in patterns of looking backward with regret and sadness, this book has already begun inviting you to turn around and face forward. Now it urges you to a second possibility: Since you're facing forward anyway, go ahead—get ready to fly.

CHAPTER THREE

Making the Choice to Grow and Change

FROM THE RUINS OF YOUR FORMER LIFE, NEW OPPORTUNITIES

*We must become
the change we seek in the world.*
—Mahatma Gandhi

Divorce presents us with a wide range of emotions, often mixed together at the same time in confusing ways. We may find ourselves praying for a quick settlement or about specific aspects of the legal process. It may seem that our prayers have been answered; it may also seem that they've been ignored.

When your divorce became final, how did you react? What was

your primary set of emotions on that day? Did you experience a great sense of relief—that the process had finally reached a conclusion? Or did you sit down alone somewhere and cry for a while, mourning the loss of everything that might have been? How did you feel on that day?

We may be glad to receive primary custody of our children, or we may be upset that our partner has taken advantage of us financially. Our emotions vary widely; we may be surprised at the sudden intensity of our responses.

One of the primary reactions many divorced persons report is an emerging sense of jealousy. Although the reasons may vary, this jealousy often arises out of a perception that the former partner is getting a "new life," perhaps by marrying someone younger, or by seeming to escape from their former duties and responsibilities as a committed partner and parent.

Not uncommonly, a wife being divorced feels abandoned and alone, resentful of her husband's opportunity to simply reinvent himself, start over, maybe even begin a whole new family.

Yet it may be the man who is "left behind," mourning the loss of true love as his former partner seemingly runs away with another. The abandoned spouse, staying in place to pay the bills, manage the debts, and continue the employment, may feel betrayed, isolated, and jealous of the apparent freedom the fleeing partner gets to experience.

Yet instead of a paradigm centered on jealousy, abandonment, and lost opportunity, it is possible to see divorce in a completely different way—as a chance to grow, as an opportunity for self-development and self-expression that might never have occurred within the context of the former marriage.

Does this mean that a woman *should* divorce—so she can express herself? Of course not! Yet it does reveal a truth about the reality of separation: There is now a whole new set of opportunities waiting to be discovered and explored.

Among those opportunities is a chance to grow and develop in ways that might have been set aside, postponed, or ignored altogether if the marriage had survived. From the ruins of the former relationship and lifestyle, new growth and possibilities may emerge. Exploring these options is one possible benefit that can be drawn from an otherwise negative experience.

What Helps a Garden Grow?

The writers of this book are both gardeners—but not the hyper-successful types who enter trophy roses in the annual contest, naming new varieties after themselves and landing their photos on the cover of *Rose Weekly*. We are gardeners by hobby and for delight, not for the passionate pursuit of prizes.

David explains that gardening is his preferred form of therapy. This is most certainly true. He experiences a deep serenity and a sense of calmness while gardening—digging into the soil seems to both restore his soul and quiet his spirit in useful ways.

Lisa enjoys the beauty and the color of the garden, plus the aromas that result when our flowering bushes are at their peak. (It's just past the ginger season here. For several weeks, every time we walked out our front door we were awash in the scent of fresh ginger—pure, natural, and invigorating.)

We are gardeners because we enjoy spending time outdoors and love the challenge and the rewards of planting, watering, trimming, pruning, and weeding. And as gardeners, we understand the basic principle of wise preparation of the soil, if one wishes to have a fruitful display of flowering beauty. From our experience, we have a question for you: Guess what helps a garden grow?

Manure.

We buy *bags* of it for our garden. It does seem kind of silly to exchange good money for manure—yet we know from years of gardening that working it into the soil will result in rich growth that would not otherwise occur. It adds nutrients and natural fertilizer that the dirt and clay in our garden does not otherwise contain. When manure arrives, growth happens.

Now comes the good news. When you get divorced, all the manure is free!

Not at the garden store, but in life. Nothing dumps manure on your prospects like a sudden divorce; nothing stinks up your life like a custody battle or a fight over finances. As a divorced person, you probably hate the "smell" of the whole process, and you may walk away feeling like you are personally tainted by the aroma. Yet instead of wallowing in the refuse and waste of your former life, perhaps there's another way of seeing it.

Try viewing the "manure" of divorce as the fertilizer for your new self. Imagine yourself as a plant growing on the border of the patio, needing some nutrients and fertilizer that have till now been missing in your life and experience. You'll discover that this paradigm shift is rooted deeply in the soil of a puzzling reality: Adversity and hardship enrich your life in ways you might not have sought. And the process can promote growth, fruitfulness, and harvest in your life.

Expanding Your Skill Sets and Capabilities

Carol didn't see her divorce coming. Busy raising her two young children, she believed her husband's emotional withdrawal from her was probably the result of his being too busy at work. Or perhaps he was simply fleeing the constant demands of two young sons who were highly active and who each faced childhood health challenges.

"He had arranged everything to his own advantage, down to the last detail...He'd calculated exactly how he would do this." In other words, Carol faced a sudden pile of manure.

Although Carol was leading the household mostly alone, she never expected to be doing so full-time. Yet one day, her husband of seven years told her he was leaving. "He said he had tried, but it wasn't working," is how Carol remembers his words on that Sunday. "He said it wasn't fair for me to be 'trapped' in a marriage that didn't have love in the middle of it. And since he didn't love me, he couldn't go on keeping me 'trapped' like that."

It was obviously her husband who felt "trapped." His actions did not appear to be rooted in concern for his wife or his two sons. Carol—stunned, uncertain, and without wise advice to guide her—mostly consented to the divorce and its terms. As a result, her ex-husband benefited financially in ways that were neither appropriate nor fair.

The settlement left her unable to care for herself and her two sons. Once she realized the new conditions she was facing, she was fiercely angry. "By the time I woke up, it was too late! He had arranged everything to his own advantage, down to the last detail. Apparently he had been planning this for a long time, so he'd calculated exactly how he would do this."

In other words, Carol faced a sudden pile of manure.

Her response to the disaster surprised even Carol herself. "I had done some accounting work while I was in college," she explains. "Nothing very complicated. It had been ten years since that experience, but in the days and weeks after the divorce, one of my first thoughts was, maybe I can dust off my old accounting skills and earn some money for us."

With the help of a friend at church, Carol developed a resumé. Her job experience was minimal and seemed out of date; the entire resumé took up barely one page. It mentioned her two years at a community college, her courses in accounting and finance, and her prior work experience, even though it was already a decade or so in the past. Aware that her resumé was thin and her prospects looked dim, she turned to her large suburban church as a pool of possible employers.

"I placed a small ad in our weekly church classifieds," she recounts. "The ad didn't try to oversell my abilities. I just said I was a newly divorced mom with two young sons to raise, and I hoped to find some part-time or full-time accounting work."

The first two weeks the ad ran, there was no response. Carol was depressed and upset; she gathered a few close friends to help her pray about finding the right job with the right terms and benefits. Then, on the third weekend that the ad ran, she was called by two prospective employers.

"I went to work 24 hours a week, for eight dollars an hour," she sighs. "It wasn't many hours, and the pay wasn't enough to care for my family. But it was better than doing nothing. Immediately, as soon as I started working, I also noticed that I felt better about myself as a person. I'm not sure why that was true, but it was. When I got that first paycheck, which frankly wasn't very large, I felt a whole lot better about who I was as a person. I felt more 'successful' than I'd felt since the divorce started."

In Carol's case, the 24-hour workweek became a full-time position within three months' time. She was grateful for the expanded opportunity, and glad also when her new boss, the owner of a small business, raised her pay to nine dollars an hour.

"I was still working cheap." She smiles. "But let's face it, as 'dusty' as my resumé was, and as long as it had been since I worked, my boss was a godsend. I kept on being grateful he even considered hiring me."

Carol's next ad in the church classifieds was for a household nanny, someone to be available in the afternoons when her sons came home from school. "I interviewed probably a half-dozen college girls, and they all seemed so...*young!*" she comments. "I suppose to them, I probably seemed old."

After several weeks of interviews, Carol hired a college girl from church to be her household helper, a decision that made her transition to a 40-hour week simpler to manage. "After a while, she began to do some cooking." Carol grins. "And she turned out to be a better cook than I was. So I'd get home from a tough day at work, and she'd have soup or something already going on the stove. We'd all sit down and eat together, then she would drive home and I'd manage the boys."

It may not have been an ideal arrangement, but for Carol it was all about survival. Brushing up on her accounting skills, preparing a resumé, and getting hired for a job all helped her cope with the loneliness, poverty, and difficult parenting tasks she faced. Obviously, though, paying a part-time nanny took a large bite out of her paycheck. So does she recommend her choice to other divorced mothers?

"Having April there when I came home," she says, "was maybe the best thing about that whole arrangement. Just to walk in the door to *someone*—not that my kids aren't people—but to walk in the door to a live adult human being, someone who asked about my day—that really helped and encouraged me. Yes, I would recommend it. But I also realize that April was God's gift to my boys and me. So although it was a choice, it was even more a gift from God."

Other divorced moms report similar blessings from amid the wreckage of their former marriages and families. Debbie, still in her 20s when divorce caught her unprepared, returned to a previous career in home decorating.

"I'd always had an eye for that," she notes, "but when I got married,

I also got pregnant right away. I didn't work outside the home for the three years Greg and I were together."

Suddenly divorced, Debbie returned to her previous employer and asked for a job—any job—that would help her return to home decorating or anything similar. She recalls being nervous about the whole prospect: "I had enjoyed that job a lot, but after all, it had been three years," she tells us. "So it was hard to walk back in the door and tell the whole world I was coming back…because my marriage had just fallen apart.

"At first my boss just told me she'd watch for a job that might fit, and she'd call me if anything came up. By the time she actually did call, I had almost given up on hearing from her."

Debbie rediscovered a first love. "I absolutely love anything about home decorating. But of course I was willing to put all that aside when I got married. Greg and I were hoping to have children right away—and we did—so that was why I chose not to work during our marriage. And Greg kept insisting he didn't want me working outside the home. So I didn't."

Debbie's story is similar to the stories of many others. Yet not everyone returns to a former employer or role—many divorced women suddenly discover new areas of interest, or they start to develop new aspects of their identity.

Developing New Interests and Rediscovering Former Ones

"I'm a divorce cliché," Lydia says laughing as we sit down near her desk in a busy office. "My husband divorced me, and I needed to find a job right away, so I became a real-estate agent!"

We smile as Lydia motions us toward two chairs by the side of her well-organized cubicle. New homes are being constructed at a rapid pace in this section of her town in California; existing homes appear to be selling strongly, and for high prices, she tells us.

"I can't tell you how many divorced women I know who are doing this," she continues. "But there are a lot of us! Just in this office, I'm one of about a half-dozen women who got into real estate after getting divorced."

We ask Lydia about the process of becoming an agent and about the level of difficulty or adversity she faced as she started her new career.

"My biggest surprise was how expensive it is," she admits. "Between the courses and the exam and the fingerprinting, and after paying all the start-up costs and buying my supplies, things really added up in a hurry. Then on top of that, I was required to join several associations at the national, state, and county level. Each of those groups has annual dues to pay, and none of them are cheap!"

How did Lydia afford all these costs in the midst of responding to a divorce she had not anticipated? How was she able to afford such high expenses as she cared for her two children alone?

"My parents." She smiles. "My parents covered all the costs of getting started. They kept telling me it was a loan, but when I tried to repay them, they wouldn't let me pay any of the money back."

We are not certain we should ask specific financial questions, but then Lydia volunteers the information we're most curious about.

"I made about $18,000 in my first full year as an agent," she sighs. "And I'm talking about my gross commissions, before taking out all my expenses. If my parents hadn't covered all of my start-up costs, I probably would have lost money—especially with the high cost of gasoline in this state.

"I made $42,000 or so my second year," she continues. "Things began to pick up—and I didn't feel quite so 'new' all the time."

What about this current year, Lydia's fifth year as a working real-estate agent?

"I'm on pace to make about $70,000 this year," she notes. "I set a goal of $100,000 for the year, but I'm not going to make it. Right now the market is really starting to slow down."

Would Lydia recommend real estate to divorced persons, especially women, as they cope with living alone and raising their children if they have any?

"Well, there are a lot of us out here doing it," she replies. "So I think that speaks for itself. Real estate is a really 'open' field—it's not that hard to get into, and companies are hiring new agents all the time. Just look at the newspaper on any given Sunday: You'll find dozens of ads for offices that are trying to hire new agents.

"But what I would tell people, especially a woman who is just getting through the hassles of a divorce settlement, is that it takes a lot of money to start up and get your business going. And you have to be patient— it isn't like you're suddenly going to start making all kinds of money. It may be six months, or even longer, before you earn and get paid your first commission.

"So you need to be sure you can get by for a long time, until the business is able to support you," she concludes. "I couldn't have done it without my parents, and I think most divorced women probably don't have the 'deep pockets' that it takes to get by while you wait for your income to start."

Lydia's manager stops by, so we pose a question about divorced women in the real-estate workplace. The manager, a well-groomed woman who looks a youngish 60 or so, smiles at the question.

"I can't confirm this with any hard data, but I've been doing this about 20 years—basically since *my* first divorce—and I'd estimate that about a third of the people selling real estate are divorced women."

So is real estate a great career choice for a suddenly divorced person?

"Absolutely!" the manager smiles broadly. "When you own your own business, the sky is the limit! You can work as hard as you want, and you're in control of your own destiny. It's a great job for anyone, but especially for a woman trying to recover, financially and emotionally, from the shock of a divorce."

Lydia nods in agreement.

"It's been a godsend for me," she comments. "That, plus my parents' willingness to support me until I could get established. I wouldn't have made it without God's help and my parents' financial help during the early days."

Depending on the office and the company, a new real-estate agent may be able to work flex-time, allowing her to manage the schedules of her school-age children, being home when most needed to run the household and care for the kids. Also, much real-estate work can be done from home, such as researching properties by computer and calling new or prospective clients by phone.

Renee discovered a new interest in the days and weeks after her divorce, something she'd always considered but never pursued.

"I'm teaching art at the community college," she tells us over a tall soy latte. "I've always had this idea in the back of my mind that someday I'd love to teach art to adults. Not that I don't enjoy middle-schoolers"—she laughs—"but in the back of my mind, I've always thought it would be fun to help adults express their creative side through art.

"I would never have pursued this if Donnie hadn't left me," she continues. "I had to find work, so I sat down with the paper and just started reading through all the ads, looking for *anything*. When I got to the 'E' section, for 'Education,' there was an ad for teaching night classes at our local community college. Although they didn't list art as one of their needs, I decided to fill out an application, meet the staff, and see if maybe there was an opening."

There wasn't, but Renee didn't get discouraged. "I had nothing to lose," she remembers. "Filling out the application and meeting the assistant dean was a learning experience for me, very valuable. So I just told myself that if God wanted to open a door in this area, then God would."

Four and a half months later, the door opened. Renee began her new career as an art instructor by teaching two classes a week, one in the afternoon and one in the evening. For Renee, with two young children at home, the amount of work and the timing of it were nearly perfect. "I had no trouble getting sitters for the evening. And I was able to find several high-school girls who were available in the afternoon. So if one of them was busy, another one could come over and sit.

"I was nervous as a teacher, at first," she admits. "I felt awkward standing in front of the class those first few sessions. I mean, I'd never really taught anything before. I wasn't sure I could do it. But I thought, *How am I ever going to find out unless I try it?*"

Renee tried it and ended up loving it. "I'm teaching a full load now," she says. "With my kids in school, I have more time available. One of the best things about community college is that classes are offered on flexible schedules—for working adults as well as the college students—and that ends up being a blessing for the instructors too."

Does she earn enough to feed her family?

"Sure...if we don't eat much." Renee laughs. "Especially when I started, with just those two classes, I wasn't earning very much money. But the point is, I was working, trying something new. In a way, I was fulfilling a dream that had been welling up within me for a long time. So, yes—we were getting by financially, in a dirt-poor sort of way. Things were tight. But I think every divorced woman knows what that's like—

and probably divorced guys do too. I mean, who is divorced and has money to spare? Nobody I know!"

Although these options might have been discovered and explored within the context of a healthy, fulfilling marriage relationship, the reality is that the shattering of a marriage union often provides the context for the discovery of a new career, or a return to a long-abandoned one.

Whether motivated by sheer economic necessity, or loneliness, or a desire to feel successful in some arena or sphere of life, divorced people enter the workforce with a high degree of motivation. No longer able to rely on a partner for encouragement and support, they learn to rely more fully on God. They often also enjoy an increasing sense of self-esteem that flows from earning an income and providing for their family's needs.

Celia works at a grocery store, a career that began with her divorce.

"It's the only place I applied," she tells us. "And I applied there because I could walk to the store. It was right in my neighborhood."

> "It has to be God...When my first husband left me, I was so broken and so alone. I just cried out to God, asking Him to help me."

Eight years after her divorce, five years after remarrying, Celia continues to work at the same store. "It's a union job," she shares. "I make good money, and the health-care benefits are great. Although we could probably get by on just David's income, I like getting out of the house during the day.

"And I like feeling like I'm making a contribution. I don't know, there's something about getting a regular paycheck that just helps me feel better. Also, in the back of my mind, I kind of think that if this marriage ever ends—it's going great, and I think David and I will be together forever—but if this marriage ever ends, I've got a good job and good benefits, so my kids will be okay."

Did Celia consider other kinds of employment?

"I would have if the grocery store hadn't hired me," she acknowledges. "But the day I walked in, one of the cashiers had just quit. And even though I didn't have any experience, for some reason I got hired right there on the spot. I started work one day after applying. I didn't really know what I was doing, but they trained me and helped me feel like things would be okay. And by the end of the first week, I felt like I'd worked there all my life...in a good way."

How does Celia explain that kind of "instant" success?

"It has to be God," she states. "When my first husband left me, I was so broken and so alone. I just cried out to God, asking Him to help me. I knew I would have to work, but I had no idea what I should do. And really I had no skills either, so I didn't see why anybody would hire me."

Fluent in both Spanish and English, Celia believes she may have been hired because she was bilingual. She remembers the store manager noticing that. "When I started at the store, there weren't any other cashiers that could speak Spanish. But a lot of customers spoke Spanish, and they would ask questions in Spanish, and nobody was there who could answer them."

Celia believes God guided her to the store and to the job.

"I was praying one morning about what to do, and I just sort of felt God guiding me to go apply at the store. I got up from my prayer time, put on my best outfit, and walked down to the store to see if any jobs were open.

"That was eight years ago, and I'm still working there. So I'm sure that God was watching out for me. God was guiding me in what to do."

Making a Skill into a Career

When Jason's wife walked away, she left behind not only her husband but also a three-year-old son. She wanted to be rid of both, and the divorce decree granted her wishes.

Jason found himself the sole custodial parent of a growing boy, one too young for kindergarten and not quite old enough for the pre-K program in the local school district. For Jason, there was only one logical choice.

He became a stay-at-home dad.

"I was working as the main IT person at a large downtown bank," he tells us. "In fact, my job might have been one reason Shawna left me. I was pretty busy with work—50-hour weeks were normal for me back then."

All alone with the responsibility of raising a three-year-old, Jason decided the job had to go.

"My boss offered me a big raise if I would stay," he relates. "And don't think I wasn't tempted. It was a great offer. But I figured my son had already lost one parent—I wasn't going to let him lose another one. Not if I could help it."

Handy with software and hardware problems, Jason decided to open his own computer-repair business, based out of his home. "I needed something I could do in my own living room. When I was working at the bank, everybody at the office was already bringing me their 'dead' personal computers or was coming to me when something crashed. So I thought I'd have a built-in market just with the people I already knew."

We ask him how business was in the early days.

"That first year my income dropped more than half," he recalls. "I think I might have made about 30 percent of my former salary that first year. I couldn't afford to buy health insurance, so I just didn't have any—not for me, not for Shane. I hated that, but what could I do? Prices for basic coverage were unbelievable."

How did he survive?

"Honestly, my parents helped us," Jason admits. "Three or four times that first year, they wrote me a check. I was too proud to ask for their help, but they could see we needed it. They were great with Shane, too."

Eventually the business began to expand. Today, Jason employs one helper full-time and three people part-time. "Counting myself, I employ five people," he says with pride. "And all of us, even the part-time people, have health-care benefits."

Shane, three years old when his mother left him, is now an active nine-year-old who plays in a soccer league. Jason skips out on work to help coach his son's team. "I'm just an assistant coach," he says, laughing. "I don't really know what I'm doing, but it's fun to be there for Shane's games. I've got enough help with my business that I don't have to be in the shop all the time. I'm not getting rich, but I really value my freedom."

Would Jason recommend this approach for other single fathers?

He thinks for a moment. "I don't know," he replies candidly. "It's been the right choice for me, but what if it didn't work out? That first year I wasn't very successful. It was sometime in the third year before I could hire any help, before the business was really supporting me.

"I guess for me, this was the only choice I could make. I'm the only parent Shane's got—and I'm going to be there for him, no matter what I have to do."

Revisiting the Goals and Dreams of Your Earlier Life

Janet went back to college, at night.

A Christian university in her metropolitan area was offering adult degree-completion classes. Depending on the amount of college credit and life experience that a person had, in most cases the degree could be completed in 15 months.

"It totally changed my life," she shares.

Suddenly alone, in her early 30's, mother of three school-age children, Janet was stunned by the divorce and wondered how she'd survive. "We had struggled financially all through our marriage. We never seemed to have enough money—a lot of our arguments were about our spending and priorities and where the money was going. I'd yell at Ed because he spent so much money 'out with the boys' all the time. He'd yell at me— that I wasn't being a careful shopper, that I was spending too much money on household stuff."

When the divorce happened, Janet had no idea what to do. "What saved me was my MOPS (Mothers of Pre-Schoolers) group," she explains. "When my kids were that age, I got involved with a MOPS program at church. Those women became some of my closest friends. Even though I didn't stay in the program, the friendships lasted. To this day, some of the girls from my MOPS group are the closest friends I have in all the world..."

She sat down with some girlfriends and sought their advice and counsel. "They were like 'go back to school and finish your degree,'" is how Janet recalls the conversation. "And I sat there thinking there was no way on earth I could possibly afford to go back to school. I mean, what were they thinking?"

Still, Janet remembers deciding she could at least explore the option. "I filled out an online response form," she tells us. "And in just a few days, I got this big packet in the mail. The more I read about going back to class and finishing my degree, the more excited I got about trying to do that."

Ironically, or perhaps obviously, the divorce helped her qualify for the financial aid that made her education possible.

"I was like the poster child for financial aid." She laughs. "I had three kids and almost no income. The more they looked at my application, the more ways they kept finding I would qualify for help. So I got grant money, and discounts, and one scholarship that was especially for single moms. By the time the financial-aid people finished working their miracles, I could actually afford to finish my education. I was just in shock. I mean, I would never have thought I could afford a college education, especially with three kids to take care of. I just couldn't believe it!"

Over the next fifteen months, Janet's MOPS friends helped watch her children during the evening classes. "We worked out a barter system," she explains, smiling. "I would watch their kids when I could, usually during the day, and then they would watch mine during the evenings when I had to go to school. Somehow, God just worked it out so that my kids always had a place to be while I was over on campus, taking my classes."

Less than two years after filling out the online response form, Janet graduated along with a hundred or so other adults, many of them also divorced.

Janet smiles at the memory. "I shouldn't tell you this, but I dated two of the guys from my classes," she says shyly. "Honestly, I was just going there to finish my education. But when I got into my classes, I found out that a lot of us were divorced, the men as well as the women. So my classes kind of became my social life too."

Meanwhile, she graduated with a degree in business. "I had taken business classes before, a long time ago. It just seemed like the best fit for what I wanted to do."

Has the degree opened doors for better employment?

"I think it will," Janet observes. "So far I've just kept my current job, which is working as an EA (educational assistant) at a nearby elementary school. It's a great job, it's near my home, and I like the hours, so I've kept it. But right now there is a lot of talk about cutting the funding for schools, which may mean less work for EAs, or even no work at all. So I may be about to find out what my business degree will do out in the workplace."

Wasn't finding a good job the main purpose of finishing her degree?

"In a way," she admits, "but not totally. I really did it—like I said—because my girlfriends all thought I should. But then as God worked it out for me to afford school, and when I started taking the classes, what happened was that I started feeling a lot better about myself, a lot more confident. And when I walked across that stage and got my degree, there's just nothing in the world that has felt so—great!" she enthuses. "In a strange way, it almost felt better than my wedding day. I mean, this was something I was accomplishing; this was achieving a goal in my life.

"And I'm still dating one of those guys from my classes." She grins. "Neither of us is in a big hurry about anything, but we both really like each other. In fact, he said the 'L-word' (love) to me recently. So maybe while I was finishing my degree I was also finding my next husband. Who knows?"

A return to the classroom is an experience shared by many divorced persons, both men and women, who find themselves facing unexpected setbacks yet discover that these obstacles are also opportunities for new growth in their lives.

"My MOPS girls all came to my graduation," Janet says, beaming as she wraps up her story. "And they yelled and screamed for me when I walked across that stage. I have to tell you—that was one of the best days of my life, ever!"

Success—in any venue—is a great way of coping with divorce.

PART TWO

Parenting Alone—
Together and Always

CHAPTER FOUR

Losing a Partner—
Gaining Your Children's Respect

LEARNING TO SUCCEED AS THE PRIMARY CAREGIVER
FOR YOUR CHILDREN

The simple reality is this—no parent is perfect.
You will make mistakes while raising your children.
You will learn and grow from those mistakes,
and so will they.

As the mother of three young sons, Karith felt completely overwhelmed. No matter how hard she tried, no matter how much energy she expended, she just couldn't keep up with the daily challenge of caring for them. She looked forward with great anticipation to 5:30 PM, the time at which Don came home from work each day. Finally, someone else was around to help with the kids!

Then one day Don didn't come home.

It was a Friday, the start of a weekend, and he didn't walk in the door at his usual 5:30. By 7:00 he still wasn't home. Sometimes he was absent for a few hours, staying out late at night without giving an explanation. Karith had adjusted to that, reasoning that "men need their space" and that time away was good for him.

By Saturday morning, Karith was worried. Had there been a car accident? Had Don been drinking again? He said he'd quit drinking when they got married—as far as she knew, it was the truth.

The afternoon passed, then the evening. Karith didn't sleep much that night; by Sunday she was in a full panic. Surely, if her husband had been in a wreck on the way home, wouldn't someone have called her by now?

By Monday, worried sick and running on adrenalin, Karith piled the three boys into her aging Ford Escort and drove to Don's workplace. There he was—right there on the job, working as if nothing unusual had happened.

"I can't talk right now," he said as Karith approached him. "I'll call you after work, okay?"

He would call her? Why not just talk when he came home?

That was when Karith first began to realize what was happening to her: Don wasn't coming home—not that night, and not ever again. He was leaving.

His departure shattered the security of her inner world. For weeks after her husband left, she slept fitfully, tossing and turning, unable to rest. When she did sleep, nightmares haunted her dreams. She awoke bathed in cold sweat.

By the time her divorce became final, Karith was living in a constant state of panic. She didn't know how she'd survive financially. She didn't know what she'd do for a living, or where to look for a job. But most of all, she was worried about her new role as a single mother—how could she possibly succeed as a single mother, raising three sons all by herself?

Welcome to Insecurity: The World of a Single Parent

One of the greatest fears faced by a married person is this: Someday your partner will find someone else. Your partner will abandon you and run away with this other person, leaving you all alone to face the challenges of life.

For many divorced people, this exact fear has already come true. In one way or another, they've been abandoned by someone they loved. Their marriage has ended, their dreams have been shattered, and their world is now a place of pain, brokenness, and suffering. They are living a nightmare, hoping to awaken and discover that somehow this was all a bad dream—it is not really happening.

Yet single parents have another fear, and perhaps a greater one.

Angie voiced it immediately, when we raised the question. Standing at the front of a room filled with 30 or so single parents, we started with a discussion question we often use: "What's your worst fear as a single parent? What's the one thing you're most afraid of?"

Angie didn't even raise her hand. Blurting out what many were already feeling, she exclaimed, "I'm afraid of screwing up my kids!"

Heads nodded all around the room.

> Particularly for the spouse who is "left behind,"
> there may be a devastating and long-lived shattering
> of self-confidence...It tends to be most noticeable
> as a single parent struggles to gain effective control
> and management of his or her children.

"That's my worst fear too," said a divorced dad from the back.

"I'm afraid I've messed mine up already," sighed one single mom, burying her head in her hands.

"They're out of control, and so am I," was another response that day.

So now you're a single parent: Welcome to insecurity.

If there's one topic single parents worry about more than anything else, it is their deficiencies and inadequacies as parents. They worry more about how the kids will turn out than they do about their own dating and relationships, their finances, or any other critical aspect of being alone.

Time after time, group after group, this response rings true. Single parents are concerned about their ability to provide the discipline, structure, and effective parenting their children will need to grow and mature. They're afraid, like Angie put it, that somehow they are "screwing up their children."

Single dads wonder how in the world they'll raise a daughter. What do they know about parenting an adolescent female, especially one who is beginning her menstrual cycle or starting to develop as a woman? These are topics single dads don't even want to think about, let alone explain to a growing young girl.

Single moms express frustration that their sons are all energy, no brains. Why do the same lessons have to be repeated over and over, and yet still the boys in the house won't listen and don't learn? If only there were a man in the house, a single mom tends to think, then maybe her sons would pay attention and shape up.

The loss of a marriage relationship often results in a loss of confidence for one or both of the former partners. Particularly for the spouse who is "left behind," there may be a devastating and long-lived shattering of self-confidence. While this loss may be revealed in many different ways, it tends to be most noticeable as a single parent struggles to gain effective control and management of his or her children.

What is difficult to manage with two parents in the home often seems completely impossible to accomplish with only one parent on duty. As they struggle to gain some sort of control over the behavior of their children, single parents tend to fall into one of two traps related to providing discipline.

Overcontrol: The High Stress of a Single Mom

Karith, devastated by the loss of her husband, Don, fell quickly into the trap of overcontrol. Without realizing it, she felt like she had lost control of her marriage and her primary relationship. Unconsciously, she reached out to try to gain control of the most meaningful relationship she had left—her role as a mother to her sons.

"I yelled at my boys all the time," is how she remembers the days and weeks after her husband first left. "I know I yelled at them while Don was around, but after he left us, it seemed like all I did was yell. Day after day, I almost lost my voice yelling at those boys, trying to get them to calm down and behave!"

She assumed, not without reason, that the boys were acting up as a response to being abandoned by their father. While there is some truth in this explanation, it is also true that the boys' behavior can be traced to their mother's sudden attempt to micromanage every aspect of household life.

"I came down on them immediately," Karith says, recalling her actions in the days following Don's departure. "I remember telling them, now that their dad was gone, they were all going to have to be on their best behavior. Things I might have let slide before, things I might not have cared about or gotten on them about, suddenly I was yelling about all the time. I became the kind of mother I can't stand to watch or be around—the mom who is always screaming at the top of her lungs, while nothing changes!"

The more frustrated she became, the more rules she tried to impose.

As her life seemed to spin out of control, she reacted by trying to "clamp down" on the natural energy and constant activity of her growing sons. And as any single mother can tell you, "clamping down" on emerging testosterone is difficult, if not completely impossible.

In Karith's case, things went from bad to worse. "The more I yelled at them, the more they acted up. So eventually I realized that yelling wasn't working, but then I didn't know what else to try. If my anger and forcefulness weren't stopping them, what would?"

Before we take a look at the answer to that question, let's consider the other trap that single parents tend to fall into—the opposite of over-control.

Being a Friend Instead of a Parent

Jennifer lost her husband and her best friend when Garrett left her. Like many other wives facing a sudden divorce, she hadn't prepared herself for the possibility of ending up alone. It was an option she had never considered.

"Marriage is forever," she explains. "We had made a commitment to God, to each other, and to our families. We pledged our lives forever."

Forever, in Jennifer and Garrett's case, lasted just over eight years. One day Garrett seemed to be a normal husband and father—the next day he was setting up a bachelor apartment across town, complete with a big-screen TV, a fully stocked refrigerator, and an expensive new sound system.

Jennifer couldn't believe what was happening. "He spent so much money on that place!" she exclaims. "I don't know where he got all that cash. Maybe he had been saving up for a long time before he moved out, knowing what he was planning to do. Maybe he went massively into debt buying all those toys. I don't know. But wow, he set up a bachelor pad that looked like something you'd see in a magazine!"

Even before the details of the divorce settlement were negotiated, she found herself sharing custody of the children with her ex-partner. Typically, she would have the kids during the week, then they would visit their dad from Friday night through Saturday night or Sunday morning.

The children, ages four, five, and seven, moved between two worlds—a life of rules and limits and poverty at their mom's place, and nonstop weekends of dazzling videos, pizza delivery, and ice-cream binges at their dad's.

How could Jennifer compete with all that? She felt like she was losing the affection and respect of her children, so she reacted in the way many single parents tend to respond. She backed away from discipline and control, and she tried to become a friendly, youthful, "fun" presence in the lives of her children.

Her efforts failed, at least if judged by the behavior of her children.

"I couldn't control them at all," Jennifer admits. "I tried to set limits and make rules and gain a sense of order, but nothing worked. If I tried to get firm, I'd hear a chorus of—'But, Mom…' and I'd lose my nerve."

She tried to give her children a greater sense of freedom and fun at her house, since the "opposition"—her ex-husband—provided seemingly unlimited amounts of freedom and fun at his house. Of course, freedom and fun are simpler to provide for 24 hours on a weekend, than for the other six days of the week!

Jennifer tried to compete, but couldn't. "Their dad gave them no rules at all," she maintains. "And I didn't want to go that far, but I definitely backed off from being the disciplinarian. I was afraid if I cracked down too hard, my kids would prefer their dad.

"In the midst of all that, I was still angry and frustrated. I didn't understand what was happening to me, or why. I was mad at God. So the one thing I wanted to hold onto—the one thing I didn't want to risk losing—was the love and affection of my kids. They were all I had—I couldn't take it if they rejected me!"

Jennifer's approach—trying to be more "fun" as a parent, trying to be a "friend" instead of an authority figure—is often taken by the noncustodial parent. However, custodial parents, increasingly weary of fighting with the only friends they seem to have left, end up caving in and permitting misbehavior, holding onto "friendship" so that they don't risk being emotionally abandoned by their children. It's a risk they're just not willing to take.

The result? Children lose their respect for such parents.

When a parent ceases to set boundaries and enforce them, children become more and more confused, angry, upset, and rebellious. Especially as they reach or approach their teen years, they'll keep testing the limits, taking ever more daring risks, hoping—at least unconsciously—to discover a parent who cares enough to draw lines, build fences, and enforce boundaries.

We'll look at issues in co-parenting in the next chapter. Meanwhile, what if you're the parent with primary custody of your children? How can you gain the respect and cooperation of your children while you struggle to cope with the new reality of a missing partner?

Having looked at several approaches that *don't* work, let's turn our attention to some of the characteristics of effective discipline—drawn from educational theory, from godly counsel, and from the personal experience of literally hundreds of single parents who have blazed these trails before us.

Five Characteristics of Effective Parental Discipline

Setting Boundaries

Your primary task as a parent, particularly if you are parenting alone, is to *set boundaries* for your children. You should do so as clearly as you can, and in ways that are age-appropriate for each child. Having your children restate what they hear is one way to be sure you're communicating. Let your children repeat your rule statements back to you. Listen to them.

Do you want their rooms to be clean? If so, how clean and how often? What, exactly, do you mean by "clean"? Be specific. If you want to see the carpet on the floor of your teenager's bedroom (more about teens later), then state clearly that "clean" means nothing strewn around on the floor, in sight.

Do you want your toddler to put all his toys back in the toy box, or perhaps the closet, at the end of the day? State this rule clearly and simply. Point the way to the toy box, or to the closet. Add an evening ritual (more about this in the next section) during which you inspect the room, searching for toys that are out of place.

Do you want the homework completed before other activities, such as Game Boy, can begin? If so, make this rule extremely clear. In addition, be sure that you personally have custody of the device so that, after inspecting the homework to be sure it's complete, you can distribute the game cartridge or control module to the child who has finished his studies.

Do you want to have rules about how clothes are cared for? Be sure to be age-appropriate (young children are not usually neat freaks, although the few exceptions are interesting to raise!). If you want certain clothes hung up on hangers, say so, pointing the way to hangers and where they should hang.

Do your children have chores that they are expected to complete? If so, do you want those chores performed at a regular time during the day or week, or do you simply want them completed by a specific deadline? Again, be simple, direct, and clear. Establish boundaries you are comfortable with, and state those boundaries with simplicity and clarity, having your children repeat them.

Monitoring Boundaries

Next, your task as a parent is to *monitor the boundaries* and to notice, in a timely and immediate way, if your rules are being ignored or broken. If you have a homework-before-Game-Boy rule, for example, it's not adequate to pass by your son's room, pause in the doorway, and ask your game-playing son if his homework is done.

"Sure, Mom!" is likely to be his response. There is even a possibility his statement will be true—but it probably won't be.

If, however, you physically inspect the homework, review it with him, maybe even check the math (let's not stretch your teaching abilities too far, unless you're gifted), then you are establishing the fact that you not only *have* boundaries, but you also *monitor* them.

There is absolutely no point in having boundaries and rules unless those rules and boundaries are backed up by timely and consistent monitoring. For instance, do you want everyone's room to be clean, once a week, at a certain time? If so, you can be certain that most or all of your children will "clean" their rooms about ten minutes before the deadline occurs. If you are using a once-a-week-the-room-is-clean rule, begin a habit of inspecting the rooms about one hour (depending on the child's age) before the deadline.

"Oh my goodness, Jared, look at the time! It's already three o'clock Saturday afternoon! That means Mommy will be coming back in just one hour, when it becomes four o'clock, to inspect your room. Look at what still needs to be done! I see clothes on the floor, toys all over your bed, and a big mess by the door! You've got one hour to get this room looking sharp, buddy!"

You can expect an "Awww...Mom!" or an "I know, Mom!" in reply, probably with a groan or a grimace or an attempt to bargain. But regardless of the response you receive, you are sending a clear signal. The room is being inspected right now—you notice and state that it doesn't pass inspection—and there's just one hour until the deadline, at which time the room better be ready.

When you come back in an hour, the hard work has already been done. You've already mentioned the rule, reinforced the rule, and pre-inspected the room with comments about where compliance is needed. Now all that's left is to show up at four o'clock and find a clean room. And your odds of actually finding a clean room have greatly increased!

Enforcing Boundaries

Your third step is *enforcing the boundaries.*

Many single parents have at least one compliant child (God be thanked), for whom and with whom it's sufficient to complete just stages one and two, above. However, for any parent with multiple children, the stage of enforcement will not only be necessary, it will be a regular feature of your parenting time. Get used to enforcement: You'll be doing a lot of it.

Yet the good news is this—the clearer, the more consistent, and the more determined you are, the more effectively you will shape and mold your children's understanding of what is expected of them. When the boundaries don't change, when the monitoring doesn't lag, and when the enforcement keeps happening—children begin to learn. Their learning curve improves immensely when the boundaries are clearly stated, checked, and enforced.

Approaches to enforcement vary with the opinions of the parent, the age of the child, and the general temperament and character of the child. Many parents report having at least one child for whom enforcement is as simple as "making a mean face" or being stern and gruff during a verbal rebuke. Particularly with younger children, it is sometimes adequate to enforce a rule by clearly indicating that you are displeased, upset, and not satisfied. Doing this, some parents report, brings compliance (albeit belated).

If you choose this approach, however, be prepared to have your child attempt to "charm" you out of your perceived "bad mood"—rather than complying with the rule or staying within the boundary. This is why a consequence that seems rooted in emotion may not be effective with many children. Emotions vary; children learn to manipulate parents in the same way by withholding or expressing affection.

Useful consequences, adjusted in age-appropriate ways, include the withdrawal or withholding of privileges or rewards. If the chores are not completed by the assigned time, then the weekly allowance will not be given. Should the room not be clean by the assigned deadline, then there will be no TV or computer time for the rest of the evening—not even if the room suddenly becomes a priority and the child suddenly begins cleaning it.

A child who learns he can avoid enforcement by completing his tasks *after* the deadline...has just moved the deadline. Whether he knows it or not, that child has just lost a measure of respect for you as a parent. Although you stated a boundary, and although you monitored it, you broke down at the point of the enforcement. Your child—even at a very young age—recognizes this for what it is: a sign of weakness or indecision on your part. You can expect almost every child, on almost every occasion, to immediately exploit any weakness or indecision you reveal.

Weak, indecisive parents produce children who believe that the world revolves around them, adjusts automatically to them, and changes its rules based on their own behavior or opinions. Clear, consistent, effective parents produce children who understand the concept of rules, limits, consequences, and good behavior. If you were trapped on a desert island with children, which category of children would you choose?

Naturally, some single parents raise questions about negotiating with their children. If you are a highly verbal parent who enjoys the give-and-take of negotiating each rule and boundary with your child, go ahead and enjoy yourself. However, it's always best to negotiate during the first step—establishing the boundaries—rather than at later steps such as monitoring or enforcing.

When you're ready to enforce a rule that has been clearly stated and consistently monitored, it's not the time to begin negotiations about whether or not there will be consequences, or what the consequences will be. Simply stated, it's too late for that! Your children should know that negotiation at the point of enforcement is a doomed idea. It won't work: not the first time, or the second time, or the time after that. At the point of enforcement, it's too late to try and talk Mom into a weaker, watered-down rule or consequence.

In general, we do not recommend negotiation as an effective strategy for single parents. Having said that, if you want to raise a brilliant lawyer or judge, or perhaps the next president of the United States, go ahead and bargain with your child about every rule and every boundary. Maybe your child will grow up to become a skilled diplomat, a federal mediator, or a member of Congress.

Otherwise, shun negotiation in favor of boundaries that are clear and rules that are simple to understand. Be your own arbiter of "fairness"—it's not a coincidence that you're the adult in the household! With clearly understood boundaries in place, get out there and monitor compliance—and make sure your kids see you doing the monitoring.

The difficult task of enforcement is made immeasurably easier when you have clearly and consistently followed the two prior steps of communicating the rules and monitoring the boundaries. With some children, it will be enough to merely communicate and monitor. With most children, you'll need to complete all three steps: communicate, monitor, enforce. But every time you enforce, you'll be making your role as parent simpler and easier in the future.

Repetition

This leads to the fourth characteristic of effective discipline: *repetition.*

Most children, and many of us as adults, learn by repetition. How do you master a new skill on the computer, or a new program you just purchased or installed? Back in the day, you might have read an instruction manual, whatever those were. These days, you'll learn by actually using the program—by repeating the tasks you use the program to perform.

> You are repeating a cycle that teaches your children what is expected of them. At a deep psychological level, this is comforting and reassuring to them.

The more times you open a file in Microsoft Publisher, the better you'll understand how to use the program. The more times you upload a digital photo from your camera to a Web-based album site, the faster you'll get at completing the steps. Just like your children, you also tend to learn by repetition.

Still not convinced? If you're over 40, can you sing most or all of the *Gilligan's Island* theme song? If you're twenty-something, can you name everyone on *Friends*—not just the characters' names, but also the names of the actors?

You have these skills, and other skills like them, because you learn by repetition. Your children learn in the same way. As you repeat your boundaries, as you monitor the rules to be sure they're followed, as you enforce some age-appropriate consequences if those rules are broken, you are repeating a cycle that teaches your children what is expected of them. At a deep psychological level, this is comforting and reassuring to them. It helps them understand their correct place in the family system and in the household.

Your children will be and will become the kind of kids other adults are comfortable being around. Teachers, Sunday-school workers, camp counselors, and others will be grateful to you. Further down the road of life, employers and spouses will be grateful to you as well. You will have done an excellent job of raising children that behave responsibly and appropriately.

Expressing Love

Finally, be sure to *express your love* to your children. Expressions of affection and unconditional love should accompany each stage of the discipline process, from setting boundaries all the way through the cycle to enforcement.

Effective single parents set boundaries precisely because they do love their children! The healthy discipline of children includes monitoring of the rules as a way of showing children that someone cares about them and their behavior. The enforcement stage occurs as an act of love also: someone cares about the child so much that they are willing to enforce consequences as a way of helping the child learn, mature, and grow.

After enforcing a consequence, particularly with younger children, it may be useful to restate your love, while also adding that you expect a change in their behavior in the future. Doing so clarifies that you are not planning to withdraw from your children or go away because you are angry. Rather, as a loving parent, you are planning to stay involved, to keep on monitoring, and to correct them as many times as needed—because you care enough to keep on helping them.

Let's face it—it's much easier in the moment to ignore bad behavior than it is to correct it. Yet ignoring your children's social skills, manners, or choices is not an act of love but rather the absence of it. Do you love your children enough to care about them all the way through the cycle of effective discipline? It takes a large and generous love to expend the physical and emotional energy you'll deplete while setting the boundaries, monitoring compliance, and enforcing consequences.

Love communicates, love monitors, and love responds with consequences.

Five Characteristics of Ineffective Parental Discipline

Now that we've explored the positive side of healthy and effective discipline for single parents, let's look briefly at the characteristics of the negative discipline that often develops when only one parent is actively raising the children.

Nagging

First among these is *nagging*. Many single mothers are self-described adherents to the "nagging method." They spend great amounts of time talking to—or at—their children, usually about the same things with the same child.

"I'm constantly telling Daniel to put his dirty underwear in the hamper," says one busy single mother. "He's the only male in this house, and the rest of us don't like finding his dirty underwear on the floor or wherever he happens to leave it—sometimes in the bathroom!"

Other single moms relate similar examples. "Jason leaves the cereal out," says one mother. "Every morning he gets the box of cereal out of the cupboard, pours himself a bowl or sometimes two, then he runs off to get ready for school. He leaves the cereal box open out on the counter. I tell him over and over again not to do that—but he still does it!"

This mother's frustration is visible. The situations vary—dirty underwear, abandoned cereal—but the themes are consistent. Each of these mothers is using an ineffective means of parenting—nagging the same child about the same issue, time after time. How do we know this method is ineffective?

It's simple: The dirty underwear is still on the floor.

Nagging involves *talking* about boundaries rather than *setting* them. Nagging is about wishing there were boundaries but constantly noticing that, in actual practice, none exist.

Nagging is basically a form of complaining. Children may not like to hear complaining, but they get used to it. After all, complaining doesn't mean anything because boundaries have not been set, monitored, or enforced. After a while, Mom's nagging just becomes "background noise" as the child goes on his way. Mom is basically training her children to "tune her out" and ignore her.

Yelling

When nagging fails, the next step usually involves *yelling*.

Yelling is a form of nagging done at a louder volume, in the false hope that now—because the noise is louder—children will now pay attention to the whining and complaining of the afflicted parent.

This fact explains in part the popularity of the ubiquitous iPod. No wonder children run around with earphones in their ears, or talking on their cell phones all the time. The atmosphere in their home is being polluted by noise. Someone is yelling at them again. *Wow—this is unpleasant—but hey, I can plug in my headphones and listen to some tunes.*

Few attempts at discipline cause a greater loss of respect for the parent than yelling. When a parent adds high volume and angry emotions to nagging and complaining, the child realizes what everyone else can clearly see: The parent is "losing it"—meaning, among other things, losing the battle for effective control of the household. A parent who resorts to yelling is more or less telling everyone, at a very high volume, "Hey, everybody look! I'm a complete failure at this!"

This may be sad, but most children don't begin complying with rules out of pity for or sympathy with the failing parent. Instead, they choose to retreat further into whatever forms of escape are available to them. Who wants to spend any time around "Old Yeller"?

Threatening

When yelling fails, as it usually does, the next unhealthy step tends to be *threatening* punishment. Ineffective single parents frequently threaten their children with dire consequences and disastrous types of punishment. But as the children quickly realize and everyone else can plainly see, none of these sad outcomes will occur anytime soon.

"If you don't stop that right now, you're grounded!" a frustrated parent may yell at an errant child. But grounded from what? And for how long? And when, exactly, is the grounding going to begin?

Idle threats, voiced in anger and frustration, not only fail in gaining control and compliance, they actually achieve just the opposite. Threats of doom and gloom, yelled at a child across a crowded minivan or from one room of the house to another, confirm to the child that—in reality—nothing bad at all is actually going to happen. The child merely learns that Mom is angry right now. Where's the surprise in that? By the time a child's parents have gotten divorced, a child is used to seeing Mom, Dad, or both get angry and stay angry. From the child's viewpoint, anger may be the normal emotional state of one or both parents.

Threats voiced in frustration do little or nothing to effectively change bad behavior. Every time an empty threat is yelled across the room, the child simply learns that the parent is in a bad mood and should be avoided for a while. If possible, the child will withdraw to another room or another activity, or into an inner world of dreams, fantasy, and make-believe.

More to the point, threats fail to communicate love. There's a huge difference between a loving parent carefully enforcing a clearly defined rule—and an angry parent making loud threats and fruitless vocal attacks.

Blaming

This is why many ineffective parents progress onward to *blaming*.

Although the most common and obvious scapegoat for blame is the ex-partner, any source of blame will do. Obviously, the household is not running smoothly or well. So whose fault is that?

The blaming single parent accuses the ex-partner of "ruining the kids" or the children themselves of being "hopelessly spoiled." Blaming becomes yet another way to complain, as the ineffective parent seeks pity and sympathy in response to an evident lack of control.

"She's always been that way," says a single mom about her four-year-old daughter, Cynthia, who throws loud, angry tantrums at school, at church, and in Wal-Mart. "She's been an exceptionally difficult child from the day she was born!" In other words, claims the blaming parent, the fault doesn't lie with any "bad parenting" on my part. Rather, the fault is the child's—Cynthia is just one of those "difficult" kids who are impossible to manage. Or perhaps her ex-partner has simply "spoiled" Cynthia so she's unmanageable.

This strategy fools no one, except perhaps the blaming parent. What is evident to grandparents, teachers, bus drivers, and neighbors is simply this: Cynthia's mother has never learned how to control her children.

Retreating

The final stage of ineffective single parenting involves some form or degree of *retreat*. This is why crowded restaurants are often the scene of major theatrical displays by unruly children. Young children wail at high volume for long periods of time, for no reason other than that they are displeased.

Older children roam the aisles of the restaurant or theater, talking loudly or making noise. While everyone else is annoyed or upset, Mom seems oblivious. This is because the ineffective single parent, exhausted from nagging, yelling, making threats, and blaming others, has decided to withdraw and give up.

In essence, this mother has decided not to parent anymore. Although the consequences will be miserable, especially for everyone else nearby, the mother has decided it's easier to do nothing (after all, yelling didn't work) than it is to learn how to gain effective, constructive, healthy control of a growing child. Single dads make the same choice, and they sometimes make it sooner.

Effective discipline is a lot of work. It's an investment of time and energy that seems never-ending. In many cases, the early results are discouraging. We should not be surprised when our children learn by ignoring the boundaries, breaking the rules, and receiving the consequences. After all, we adults tend to learn in the same way—by repetition. As you keep on repeating good practices and healthy approaches to parenting, you will move in positive directions, one step at a time. Parenting is a journey, not an arrival. Journey wisely.

Hallmarks of Healthy Discipline

Here are some identifying traits of effective single parenting:

1. *Set.* You set clear boundaries, explaining the rules to each child in age-appropriate ways.

2. *Monitor.* You consistently monitor those boundaries; you notice if a rule is tested or broken.

3. *Enforce.* When your rules are challenged or ignored, you enforce the consequences.

4. *Repeat.* Most children learn by repetition. Keep on being clear and consistent; it's your best hope of gaining and keeping control.

5. *Love.* Before and after the consequences are enforced, you let your child know that he or she is loved and valued.

Hallmarks of Unhealthy Discipline

Here are some identifying traits of ineffective single parenting:

1. *Nag.* You constantly give the same instructions to the same child, over and over again.

2. *Yell.* You express your anger by raising your voice; you lose control of your emotions.

3. *Threaten.* You often repeat a threat about what will happen unless you are heard and obeyed.

4. *Blame.* You complain about your situation—how difficult your life is, or how little help you receive from others, including your children and your ex-partner.

5. *Retreat.* Unable to get compliance, you withdraw from the situation, deciding not to notice unacceptable behaviors.

SINGLE PARENTING SERIES
The Center for Marriage & Family Studies
Del Mar, California

CHAPTER FIVE

The Delicate Dance of Co-Parenting

DIFFERENT RULES, DIVIDED LOYALTIES, POTENTIAL CONFLICT

When a divorced couple stops fighting long enough to think about the kids, everyone can benefit. Some divorce relationships actually function more smoothly than the marriage that preceded them.

After a divorce becomes final, there are fewer things to fight about than there were during the marriage. Now that you and your ex-partner have set up separate households, this means that each of you can manage and spend money the way you choose, set the thermostat at the temperature you prefer, and flip through the channels with your very own remote control. Would you like to repaint the bathroom in a lively shade of purple? Go right ahead—it's up to you.

In these ways, divorce can be liberating. Finally, you do not have to make allowances for the taste, preferences, habits, and eccentricities of another adult. You can pretend the fast-food commercial is now your new lifestyle: You can "have it your way!" This can be briefly intoxicating, particularly if you've tried very hard, all during your marriage, to serve and please the taste and whims of your spouse. Now, suddenly, there's no one around to impose their preferences or to oppose your ideas about how things ought to be done.

Yet although there are fewer issues to fight about, you may discover that the fights that do occur are deeper, more intense, and more difficult to resolve. This is because instead of disagreeing about trivial things, now you are at war over issues one or both of you may care very deeply about.

Such as how your children will be raised.

"I didn't think my son should be watching R-rated videos as an 11-year-old," Sarah says, quite reasonably. "I didn't think we should be buying him violent games for his XBox. Things he might be able to sort out and deal with later, as a 19-year-old, were too early for him at age 11, in my view."

Sarah's ex-husband, Grant, saw it differently. "He's a guy!" Grant said, not sensing any problem. "It's not like he can't see this stuff all the time anyway at his friends' houses and on the Internet!"

For Grant, there was nothing to be concerned about. He rented and watched R-rated videos and allowed his son to do so also. These included, as Sarah would later learn, violent horror and slasher films that seemed to center on every kind of gory and graphic murder—exactly the type of visual images she wouldn't choose for her son.

In the battle for the mind and imagination of a soon-to-be-teenage boy, she hoped her church's youth group, including the new youth pastor who took the teens snowboarding and paint-balling, would be a primary factor in shaping and molding her son. She hoped videos like The Lord of the Rings series would attract her son's interest, calling him to values like honor, loyalty, and courage.

Instead, while she did her best to model Christianity for a growing boy whom she saw as young and impressionable, her ex-husband seemed to have no discretion at all in what he rented, viewed, or showed to his son.

"Hey, he's watching this stuff with me," Grant insisted. "After all, it's not like he's out there on the street, getting into trouble or something."

Sarah and Grant's battle over what their son could or could not view and experience played on for more than a year without a satisfactory resolution. Their struggle echoes similar conflicts faced by ex-partners, particularly if one of the parties is concerned with and passionate about raising their children in a community of faith, according to a "higher" set of values or principles.

Influence, Authority, and Control

Divorce is a great teacher, even if the lessons aren't always pleasant. One of the first things divorce teaches you is, you are not in control. You may have wanted your marriage to last forever—it did not. You may have hoped to have a loving family, yet it turned out that you and your partner were better at fighting with each other than you were at loving each other.

> Divorce is a giant billboard along the highway of life.
> As you pass by, you can't help but read the
> message emblazoned across the sign's surface:
> YOU ARE NOT IN CONTROL.

You may have done everything in your power to build a marriage based on sharing a common faith and a deep commitment to spiritual values—but despite your best efforts, this kind of unity never emerged in your relationship. Maybe you were the only one who was committed to spiritual growth, nagging your partner to attend church, get involved in a small group, or start reading the Bible. You hoped, you dreamed, you prayed—yet nothing changed.

Divorce is a giant billboard along the highway of life. As you pass by, you can't help but read the message emblazoned across the sign's surface: YOU ARE NOT IN CONTROL. This is not a "fun" lesson, but it can be a useful one.

One day you discover that this same truth—*you are not in control*—applies to your children. You learn that—despite everything you are teaching and training your children, despite every moral value and character trait you are hoping to instill in them—your ex-partner is modeling or even recommending a lifestyle that is completely different, perhaps decadent or immoral.

How can you respond to this type of challenge? How should you relate to your ex-partner in the process of making decisions about your children? As we consider the delicate dance of co-parenting, here are some of the key guidelines recommended by those who are learning the lessons every day.

It's Your Household: Make Your Own Rules

Clarice is absolutely firm on this one. "It's essential," she insists. "You can't let your ex-partner, your good friends, your parents, or someone else keep sticking their nose in your business all the time. You've got to decide—for yourself—how you're going to run your household, and *especially* how you're going to raise your kids!"

Heads nod affirmatively around the room as other single parents indicate their approval of Clarice's statement.

"I have to agree," Gary concurs. "One of the things my ex-wife and I fought about all the time was how to discipline our kids. But now that each of us has our own household and our own life, I think it's important that both of us can raise our children the way we see fit."

Gary sees no particular contradiction in this statement. "My house, my rules," Gary asserts. "Her house, her rules."

Clarice rejoins the discussion. "That's what I'm saying," she reiterates. "How can you possibly let your ex-partner dictate what your rules are going to be? I mean, the marriage is over. Any sort of power or authority the other person may have had over you and your choices went away when the marriage did."

There's an edge in her voice that many seem to notice.

"I'm not sure it's about authority so much," Marie inserts gently. "But I think many of us in this room are finding that our ex-husbands, or our ex-wives, have very different values than what we have. So it's really a case of supporting our own values, of providing the right kind of environment for our kids—even if the rest of the world, and the school system, and their dad (or mom) goes another way.

"I think God expects us to teach, explain, and model what we believe about the world and about how people should live," she continues. "And since my ex isn't even a believer at this point, if my kids are going to see God or hear God in their daily lives, it's going to have to be at my house."

We ask what that means in practical terms.

Marie is quick to respond with her answer. "I know my kids are watching what their dad does, and how he lives," she says deliberately. "And I also know they're watching me. I gave up trying to be perfect a long time ago. I just can't do it! But I can keep God at the center of my attention. I can make prayer a big part of our life together as a family. I can be actively involved in my church, showing my kids that my values include serving and ministering and caring for others.

"I think—I have to believe this—I think over time my kids are going to be old enough to see the contrasts and the differences between their dad and me. Does that sound prideful? I don't mean it that way. What I mean is, eventually my kids are going to see the difference between selfish and unselfish, between seeking your own pleasure and trying to serve others.

"I can't make their choices for them, and I can't be sure they'll be smart enough to make wise decisions. All I can do is try to show them what I value, what I care about, what I believe—and that's what I'm doing every day."

There is silence in the room for what seems like several minutes.

Then Gary rejoins the discussion. "That's way beyond what I was talking about," he admits. "I just meant that each one of us can set our own rules about bedtime, about eating candy, about what friends they (our kids) can see and when they can see them.

"But here I am, trying to be good at discipline and shaping my kids' lives, but I'm not paying nearly enough attention to other people and their needs. I'm not doing anything—not anything at all—that shows my kids I care about other people. I've been so busy just trying to survive this whole mess…"

Around the room, other single parents are reflecting in silence on the truth and the implications of Gary's comments.

Stay Firm If Your Kids Try to Manipulate You

We share this chapter with a busy single parent, asking her to proof-read and offer any suggestions she might have. We are surprised when she laughs at the subheading just above.

"You actually wrote the phrase '*if* your kids try to manipulate you'?" our friend asks, rolling her eyes in disbelief. "Are you implying they might not? That's hilarious!" She chuckles loudly. "This section should be titled 'Stay Firm *When* Your Kids Try to Manipulate You,'" she insists.

Dealing with this reality daily, she lays claim to being an expert in this phenomenon.

Our friend, who tends toward the dramatic, gives us her best impersonations of the voices of her children.

"Dad lets me stay up as long as I want to!" she whines in a high-pitched, young-sounding voice.

"Dad says chocolate is one of the four basic food groups!" she pouts in a different cadence.

"Dad says, if I get my ears pierced, he'll pay for it!" she insists, sounding like a petulant teenager.

"There are days"—she returns to her own speaking voice—"when I think every sentence coming out of their mouths begins with 'Dad says...' or else, 'But Dad says...' So the issue is not 'if' your kids try to manipulate you, but 'when' they try to do it. Because you can be sure they'll try...and they'll keep trying."

Our friend's perspective is shared by many of those who attempt the delicate dance of co-parenting. Typically, one ex-partner believes that the other is "spoiling" or "overindulging" the children. And when there are significant differences in the level of privileges the children enjoy in the two households, you can expect them to notice those differences and to make a relentless, often concerted effort to change the "stronger" household so it functions more like the "weaker" one.

Yet despite this pressure, it is possible to defend your territory and establish your rules and boundaries as firm and unyielding.

"My ex lets them walk all over her," says Brandon about his ex-wife's style of caring for their two young children. "What's it going to be like when they're older, if she can't even control them right now?"

He expresses his frustration further. "She lets them say 'no' back to her all the time. She lets them yell at her. I've heard them calling her names—right out loud. How are they ever going to learn respect for adults, or respect for authority, when she lets them get away with stuff like that?"

Brandon serves in the United States armed forces.

"Hey," he says as we make the connection, "I'm not trying to make little soldiers out of these kids. Far from it! But I think children ought to understand that adults are in control. I think children ought to learn to respect authority at an early age. I think it's a lesson they're going to need, later in life.

"Is it respectful when a child says 'no' to an adult? I don't think so. Is it respectful when a child yells at his mother or calls her a very bad name? I don't think so. And if you let them get away with it when they're little..."

We ask Brandon if his children try to manipulate him.

"They used to," he says simply.

Is he implying they don't behave this way anymore?

"No, I'm not implying that, I'm stating it as a fact," he says crisply. "I don't put up with that in my house. I won't stand for kids trying to tell me how I ought to run my own home, or trying to tell me that their mom's way is better."

We ask him for practical advice about achieving results like this.

"My Becky is eight—she's my oldest," he says proudly. "She's been living between two houses since she was six, but she's doing really good. I'll tell you exactly what I told Becky when she started telling me about her mom's way of doing things. I said to her that if her mom had any rules that were stricter than mine, or firmer than mine, or tougher than mine—I wanted to know about it. Because if I heard about any tougher rules, I was going to start using them in my house.

"Then I told her, if her mom had any easier rules, rules that weren't as tough as mine or as firm as mine, I didn't ever want to hear about it— not even once. Never! I told her if she tried to bring up easier rules, she

would be punished for bringing that up—and I made sure she understood that I meant it. So she had permission to tell me about the rules
at her mom's house—but only if those rules were 'tougher' than mine.
Otherwise, no conversation.

"See how that works? I am giving her permission to talk about the
difference in our two sets of rules—but only if Mom is firmer than I am.
Do you think she's ever talked to me about rules since that time?"

In spite of ourselves, we smile. We have to ask the obvious question.
Has Becky told her father about any ways her mother is *tougher* than
he is, any rules that are firmer at Mom's house?

Brandon laughs out loud. "First of all, there's zero chance of that
being the case," he insists, smiling. "And second of all, if it did happen,
I'm sure Becky is smart enough not to tell me about a tougher rule. You
think she wants me to get any tougher than I am? I'm sure she's smart
enough to keep it to herself if her mom ever gets firmer than me. Not
that that's ever going to happen!"

Children as young as Becky and much younger can be expected to
notice when one parent is soft or easy. Kids can be expected to prefer
the less difficult household structure and to pressure the firmer parent
to bend or change.

When a parent gives in to emotional blackmail, that is, trying to
please a child by softening the rules, adjusting the boundaries, or changing the limits, the child learns that adults can be trained—by whining, begging, pushing, or otherwise manipulating the emotions of the
parent. This role reversal quickly places the child in control, with the
adult gradually conforming to the child's will.

If God had intended that children would rule the world, he would
have designed it so children would give birth to parents. Instead, God
appears to want it the other way. Adults are the ones who give birth,

provide nurture, and train children in the way they should go. When adults abdicate this responsibility in the face of emotional pressure from their children, it is the children who suffer most.

Divorced parents, sharing the custody and training of their children with ex-partners whose values and beliefs may vary widely from their own, are particularly vulnerable to the appeals, pleas, and bargaining of their children. Wanting the best for their children, and insecure in their role as a single parent, some of these adults eventually give in to the children's incessant pleading.

They soon regret doing so.

By standing firm in your boundaries and establishing distinct control of your own household and your own space, you help children learn to adjust, change, and be rightly related to other authorities in their lives. Later in life, as these children transition into higher education, employment, and social systems, the lessons you've taught them will help them succeed and thrive as adults.

Meanwhile, your own home will be a more peaceful place. You will have established the fact it is the parent's role to make the rules. You will have demonstrated the fact that, although your child's other parent may have different values and ideas than yours, you are the one who sets the tone and establishes the policies in your own home. Your children may protest against this, but they'll understand it. They will also understand if you give in to their pressure: They'll soon apply more of it.

Admitting Differences While Avoiding Criticism

While establishing your own household boundaries and firmly defending those boundaries against emotional manipulation and constant whining, another problem or difficulty may emerge. You may become aware that your ex-partner is living and behaving in ways that are immature, unhealthy, and unwise.

As you explore this difficulty, you'll need to be aware of your own vested interest in the matter. There is probably a natural animosity toward your ex-partner that dwells inside you since the marriage relationship became difficult. This latent or explicit hostility may distort your opinions about your ex-partner, magnifying his or her bad qualities while minimizing any positive traits.

Before acting on areas of difference, it is helpful to attempt an objective evaluation of the situation. Is your ex-partner actually behaving in a way that is immature, or are you being overcritical of him? Is your ex-spouse openly undermining your values, or is she simply living consistently with her own system of ideas and beliefs?

One of the most helpful approaches you can take, for the sake of your children, is to limit your criticism of your ex-partner. If at all possible, try not to criticize him or her as a person. This will prove difficult! After all, your divorce was probably not based on mutual admiration. Further, your former partner is almost certainly making choices you disagree with, and is perhaps having a true negative impact on the moral, spiritual, or educational formation of your children as they grow toward maturity—or at least it seems so to you.

It is possible to distinguish between conflicting values without attacking people who hold values different than your own. To some extent, this natural process comes about in any family circle, particularly when you marry into a family that expresses affection, spends money, or makes decisions in ways that are much different than the way you were raised. Rather than openly criticizing your new family members, you learn to appreciate them as persons while still disagreeing with many aspects of their choices, decisions, and values.

In other words, it is possible to practice tolerance without compromising your own views about social issues, including the raising of children. It is not necessary for you to agree with or affirm your ex-partner and his or her value system. However, again, it is healthy and positive for the children if you can refrain from openly criticizing the personal character of your ex-spouse.

Your children have probably heard you fighting. They probably realize there is deep tension between you and their other birth parent. They are uncomfortable with this tension; it increases their own levels of stress. Rather than reacting to a difficult ex-partner with anger and criticism, it is wiser and more helpful to distinguish between bad behavior and a bad person.

There may be some occasions when it is necessary to forcefully intervene on behalf of your children, particularly younger ones. For example, does your ex-partner keep pornography around his home? It is reasonable and helpful for you to privately insist that none of this material be visible or accessible to your children during their times of residence.

Since you cannot control your ex-partner and his basis for making decisions, your only route of approach will be to appeal—yet you can do so with firm conviction, especially when defending younger children against social conditioning that may affect them in negative ways. You can express your views without attacking the character of your ex-partner—and to the extent you are able to do so, you greatly increase the chance your former spouse will listen to you and will react in positive ways.

Over the long term, speaking about your ex-partner in positive ways will have a positive and helpful influence on the lives of your children. Instead of hearing bitterness and anger from you, they will be experiencing an optimistic and tolerant view of people that helps them refrain from judging others. This helps them avoid becoming critical, cynical, and caustic in their view of the world.

After a divorce, ex-partners are better at noticing faults in each other than they are at affirming strengths. Rare is the divorced couple that can maintain a civilized dignity in all conversations—public and private—about each other. Yet when an effort is made to avoid criticizing the father or mother of your children, the children gain a sense of well-being that helps them adjust to the difficult world of co-parenting and multiple households.

You may harbor strong feelings about the personal inadequacies and evident immaturities in your ex-partner. Your observations may even be readily confirmed by objective witnesses. Even so, you are wise as a person and helpful as a parent when you avoid the trap of openly criticizing and attacking your ex-spouse. In particular, you can and should avoid criticizing his or her character. If you absolutely must comment about values, keep the discussion centered on philosophies and ideas, not on persons and identities.

Competing or Cooperating?

When co-parenting is viewed through the paradigm of competition, both ex-partners may struggle to prove that their method is "best," that their household is the "most positive environment" in which to raise the children. The problem with the competition paradigm is obvious: By viewing the family through the lens of "winning" there is always a "loser"—in such cases, everyone tends to lose.

> When two parents...each take an unselfish view and place the needs of the children as a high priority, disagreements can be minimized and positive discussions can replace high-volume arguments.

When co-parenting becomes a cooperative partnership, it is possible for a divorce relationship to work more smoothly than the marriage ever did. In our work with marriages and families over the past two decades, we have encountered numerous divorced couples who had very little ground for agreement in their core values and beliefs, yet they came together in a unified way to work for the good of the children they had together.

When a parent functions unselfishly, wanting the best for the children, everyone gains and benefits. When two parents—even two parents who have decided to end a marriage union and live separately—each take an unselfish view and place the needs of the children as a high priority, disagreements can be minimized and positive discussions can replace high-volume arguments.

The authors are aware of dozens of divorced couples who fit the above description. Although many have remarried or are involved with other partners, these couples have learned to function positively and unselfishly with regard to raising their children. They have put aside their personal differences long enough to think about what is best for their kids. In doing so, they have greatly increased their children's sense of well-being, security, and personal worth.

Stay Willing to Learn, Grow, and Change Your Perspective

You won't know everything about parenting in the aftermath of a divorce. Years later, you *still* won't know it all. Despite holding strong opinions and deep personal values, stay open to learning, growing, and changing.

You may discover that, in your early years of co-parenting, you are the parent who is firmer or more structured in the way you raise your children. You may feel like the only parent mature enough to fulfill the necessary role of being the grown-up in the home. You may tire of always being the authority figure, yet you may continue to believe that it's necessary.

If so, be open to discovering the unique gifts and character of each of your children. Some of them will naturally need less structure and less discipline than others. Some of them will require enormous amounts of attention: You'll need to not only set and monitor boundaries, you'll also need to spend all of your time enforcing, enforcing, and enforcing again! As you do so, notice the ways in which each child reacts and responds to discipline and structure differently.

You may be the parent who believes that a looser and freer approach permits the child to grow and develop more naturally. As you mature and age, you may realize that a little structure is good for a child—perhaps even necessary. Be willing to adapt your thinking as the laboratory of human experience yields results that you live with every day. Don't be ashamed to change—all of us can learn!

The key factor to keep in mind about learning, changing, and growing is that you can do so at your own pace. You need not cave in to the emotional pressure of your children, your ex-partner, your parents, friends, or anyone else. While many people may have opinions to offer—and may follow through by offering their opinions to you—you are not obligated to respond by changing your views to accommodate their ideas, values, or beliefs.

If you are involved in a church, a large extended family, or some other social network, look closely at the families around you. Where do you see children who are well-behaved, well-socialized, and seem to be high achievers? Whose children seem the most confident, the most capable, the most generous?

Learn by observation. Watch how other parents treat their children; be sure you watch what they do, not what they say. Learn from other parents, and especially from single parents and postdivorce blended families, how to lovingly manage the many difficult challenges of co-parenting.

Learn by reading. Go to the library and check out books in early child development, child psychology, and learning. Apply what you learn by using your knowledge to improve your capabilities as a parent. Along the way: Stay humble. There are many "experts" who fail miserably as marriage partners and parents; your goal is not to become an expert, but to discover what works.

If your children are several years apart, you may discover you are a wiser and better parent by the time the younger ones come of age. By then you will have learned by experience, by trial and error, how to be a more effective father or mother to the unique personalities that occupy your home. By then, saturated in Scripture and blessed by observing "successful" parenting styles, you may have learned enough to consider sharing your wisdom with others.

Within a first marriage, the discipline and education of children may be and become one of the "flash points" that causes frequent arguments. You should not expect this to be any different for a divorced couple! Yet it is also true that some divorced couples actually manage the education and training of their children with more grace and aplomb than some married couples.

If you've ever seen a long-term married couple bicker and fight, you may understand this reality. Constantly arguing with and undermining each other, these long-term married partners disagree about everything, often vocally.

Freed of the constant stress of living together, some divorced couples find their way to a cooperative, reasonably unified approach to raising their children. It is not necessary for both persons to agree on everything. It is helpful, however, when both parents find the grace and good nature to be tolerant of each other's personal style, values, and ideas.

Co-parenting is a delicate dance—yet you can learn the steps and perhaps even manage a graceful turn or two during your time on the ballroom floor.

The Delicate Dance of Co-Parenting: Learning a Few Graceful Steps

Here's what other divorced parents are learning as they jointly care for the education and training of their children.

1. *Each parent determines values for their own household.* We cannot control other adults; we certainly cannot successfully control our ex-spouse. We can, however, set the tone and decide the values of our own household. Let us do so with confidence, fulfilling our responsibility to ourselves and our children.

2. *Children should respect your rules, not change them.* Your children may be "freer" at your ex-partner's home. They may enjoy more privileges, more money, or fewer boundaries there. Simply put, that home is that home; yours is yours. Stand firm and refuse to give in to emotional blackmail.

3. *Admit differences without criticizing your ex as a person.* Your children will notice and observe differences in your moral values, culture, and conduct. This is natural. If you talk about these issues with your kids, do so without criticizing their other parent as a person. Talk about issues and ideas, not about people.

4. *Try cooperating instead of competing.* Working together toward a common goal is sometimes easier if you don't have to actually live with the other person! Some divorced couples manage and oversee the care of their children more successfully and peacefully than some married couples do. Set aside your differences, be unselfish, and think of the kids.

5. *Be open to learning, growing, and changing.* You will be a wiser parent as you learn by experience. Be open to what experience may teach you, and be ready to change and grow as a person. However, do so as a conscious choice, rather than allowing yourself to be pressured by parents, ex-partners, or other well-meaning persons. Look around you for examples of parents that seem to be succeeding somehow. Watch what they do.

Chapter Six

Losing Access, Yet Gaining Influence

THE DIFFICULT WORLD OF THE NONCUSTODIAL PARENT

My dad called me on my birthday—
he said he's sending me 20 dollars.
I hope he means it.
My mom says he's been drinking again.
—Danielle, age 13, child of divorce

When Shannon left, she took her two daughters with her. Married to Tim for five years, she left on a Tuesday morning. She drove halfway across the country with her daughters, ages four and two, sitting beside her in a rusty, once-white Ford Ranger. In the back of the truck, she'd piled her clothes, her daughters' clothes and toys, and very little else.

When she got to her parents' house, she pulled the truck into the driveway and, unannounced, moved herself and her girls into what had once been her own bedroom. She stayed several months; by then she had found her way into another relationship: She and the girls moved in with her new boyfriend.

Tim, worried about his daughters and facing a seasonal layoff at work, didn't know what to think or expect. He knew Shannon didn't love him; she had explained that to him, many times. But she had never said she'd be leaving. She had certainly never said she'd be taking his girls when she left.

After she'd been gone for three days, Tim realized that she must have had someplace to go. Worried sick about his daughters but trying to sound normal on the phone, Tim called Shannon's parents, casually inquiring if he could speak with his wife.

"She's here, but I don't think she wants to talk to you," Shannon's dad told Tim. "She hasn't said much to us, but she did say it was over. She said if you called, she didn't want to talk to you."

Head over heels in debt, facing a highly probable seasonal layoff at work, Tim wasn't in a position to chase across the country and confront his wife. With the truck missing, Tim had only a motorcycle for personal transportation.

"I should have gone after them, right then," Tim says today, with the wisdom of hindsight. Instead, feeling bound to his employer and desperate to earn any cash he could before the layoffs occurred, Tim stayed where he was. He worked as many hours as the plant would give him, coming home to an empty house that was a constant reminder of the family life he had lost.

"I was crazy," he says with conviction. "I was worried sick, out of my mind with missing my little girls. By that time I realized I didn't really love Shannon anymore, although I would have stayed with her forever. But I sure loved my girls. I couldn't stand to be so far away from them!" Tim's eyes mist over with the memory.

Looking back, Tim has no idea why he didn't pursue the girls more quickly, although his options were few and seemed fewer. When he finally did hear from Shannon, she sent legal documents arranging for a separation. He saw hope in that, not realizing that for Shannon it was one step in a process that led to another destination: divorce.

"I was actually encouraged a little bit, when she sent the papers about the separation," Tim says. "To me, that meant maybe we could still work things out and get back together, at least for the girls' sake."

A Plan Unfolds

Instead, Shannon waited a while and then filed for divorce, filing also for primary custody of the children. She had planned her actions with great care, making sure that before the filing, everything was arranged in her favor. In fact, the cards against Tim were stacked so high, he couldn't even see the table. All he knew was what he felt in his heart: He was losing his girls.

By the time Shannon filed for divorce, all available evidence favored her home, her living arrangement, and her state as the best place for the girls to be raised. Although Tim hired an attorney (which he could barely afford), the lawyer was unable to work any miracles on his behalf.

With the divorce duly filed, Shannon was granted temporary custody of their two girls. Tim had "visitation rights" but was required to contact his wife, scheduling any visits in advance, giving her at least 48 hours of notice that he was coming. Because of the long distance between Shannon's home and his, Tim realized he would rarely if ever see his girls under this arrangement.

He debated leaving his job. He considered filing for bankruptcy. More than once he considered ending his own life. He was depressed and worried. Given his tenuous mental state, he might have carried out any of those actions. Instead, he decided to "get religion," in his terms.

"I guess I realized if anyone could help me, God could," he says slowly. "Or actually, I realized nobody could possibly help me—except maybe God, if there was a God."

A Faith Is Found

Although Tim claims to have found faith in the days that followed, what he actually discovered was a network of new friends, all of whom believed in his rights and duties as the father of two children. His new friends at church made it their duty to pursue his rights, study his case, and advise him about what to do.

"They kept saying they were praying for me," he remembers. "And I guess I was grateful for that, but I thought to myself, what could prayer do?"

Whether it was prayer or action, Tim's life did begin to change. "Doors opened," he says succinctly. "Before I knew it, there were possibilities in front of me that never would have happened."

A few months after finding his way to faith, he was packing his belongings into a van that belonged to some new friends. Through church connections, he was offered a job in a community less than two hours away from the town where Shannon lived. The work was similar to what he had been doing already.

Before he left, church friends from "home" helped Tim find an apartment in his new community: He'd be renting the basement of an older, retired couple who attended a church of the same denomination, there in the new community. The rent was low—better yet, the basement had two furnished bedrooms. If he was somehow able to secure any kind of visitation rights, he could offer a real bedroom in which to house his girls during their visits with him.

He made the move and began the new job. Despite being extremely eager to see his girls, Tim made no contact with Shannon during any of this time. He wanted to be fully relocated, fully moved in, and gainfully employed before he asked for his first visitation.

> "You sound a lot better," Tim's father-in-law
> told him. "And just between you and me,
> I think the girls miss you—a lot."

He planned to make the two-hour drive on a Saturday, announcing only later, after the fact, that he now lived in the same state. If Shannon could work by secrecy and surprise, Tim thought to himself, then so could he. He would show up and take his daughters to McDonald's. Surely there was a McDonald's in the town where they now lived. If not, he'd find them some ice cream somewhere.

His plan worked, mostly. When he made his first call to request a visitation on the next Saturday, he was denied permission—by Shannon. She had an excuse for why the girls were not available, so Tim immediately asked for the following weekend. Shannon could not quickly find a reason to deny his request.

His conversation was with Shannon's father, not with Shannon herself. Tim didn't know the name of her boyfriend—he didn't know how to reach his ex-wife directly. Before hanging up, her father volunteered some information. "You sound a lot better," Tim's father-in-law told him. "And just between you and me, I think the girls miss you— a lot."

Tim hung up the phone and wept.

Although he'd be waiting another week before he saw them, he now lived in the same state as his daughters! He was working, saving his money, and he had two critically important things in his favor: a good car for his daughters to ride in, and a wonderful apartment to share with them if he could get overnight custody.

It was almost more than Tim could take in, after months of being alone and worrying himself sick about losing his family. He was already actively attending church in his new community, where people knew his life story even before he arrived. People seemed to like him—they were cheering for him to gain access, even if temporary and occasional, to the two daughters who were clearly the light of his life. Now, if he could wait another few days, he would see his girls!

For Tim, those days seemed like an eternity, but they eventually passed. Saturday morning dawned bright and clear. He washed and waxed the car he'd bought; although nearly eight years old, it gleamed like new.

He pulled into the driveway of Shannon's parents' home. His daughters were waiting and watching. Both of them ran, screaming, out the front door of their grandparents' home. Shannon, who had merely dropped the girls at her parents' home, had decided not to see him in person.

Tim cried like a baby; his daughters cried also. Shannon's parents, watching from the porch, couldn't keep from weeping right along with them. It was—despite all the tears—an extremely happy reunion.

Although Shannon had insisted that the girls remain in her parents' home, her parents quickly relented and changed their instructions. When Tim asked to take his girls to McDonald's, his father-in-law quickly agreed.

"Oh, go ahead," he remembers his father-in-law saying that day. Both men were crying. "But be sure to bring them back here a little early, okay?"

Tim nodded in agreement. Moments later, he and his two daughters were munching hamburgers and french fries, desperately trying to catch up on the months they had missed, being apart. Conversation was fast and frantic. Everyone talked at once.

"I missed you, Daddy!" he remembers his older daughter telling him that day. "I missed you so much!"

For Tim, who might have been angry at his soon-to-be ex-wife for running away—and for basically "stealing" his daughters in the process—there was only joy on that Saturday, no anger or bitterness.

"I didn't care, I was just so glad to see them," he insists. "I wasn't mad at Shannon anymore, I was just glad to have my girls back, even if only for a few hours. Those few hours were the best time I'd had in almost a year."

He returned the girls ahead of schedule, taking the time to walk around his ex-in-laws' home and visit for a while. "I'm living just a few hours away," he decided to tell them, no longer worried about what Shannon knew or found out. "And I plan to be back here every week-end from now on, visiting my little girls."

His former mother-in-law actually smiled at him. "That just seems right," he remembers her saying. "That just seems right."

In the months that followed, Tim began adjusting to facts that are a daily reality for many noncustodial parents. Although wanting to house and care for his daughters, he found himself at the mercy of prior legal arrangements. Most of the time, his daughters lived with his ex-wife, her boyfriend, the boyfriend's children from a prior marriage, two dogs, and a cat.

Meanwhile, Tim lived two hours away—gloriously glad to be so near to his daughters after so many months apart, but lamenting the fact he only had Saturdays to be with his girls. In time, with the help of an attorney arranged through his new friends at church, he began having his daughters spend the weekends at his home, a process Shannon bitterly resisted.

He would drive to his ex-in-laws' home Saturday morning, pick up the girls, drive them back to his home, keep them overnight Saturday, take them to church on Sunday, then drive them back Sunday afternoon, returning to his own home by sometime Sunday evening. It was a lot of driving—eight hours every weekend—but to Tim it was worth whatever it cost in time, gas, and money.

"Those girls are everything to me," he says simply.

Many noncustodial parents, most but not all of them fathers, agree with Tim's perspective wholeheartedly.

Tales of absentee, irresponsible, immature noncustodial parents, both fathers and mothers, are numerous enough to be a cliché. Yet the story emerging from our current era is somewhat different: noncustodial parents who are making every effort to be responsible, to be considered worthy of time with their birth children, only to encounter seemingly insurmountable obstacles along the way.

"My daughter wouldn't come see me, even though we'd all agreed on the schedule in advance," one father says regretfully. "She was 11 years old by then, and I missed her terribly. But on the weekends I was supposed to have her, she would just refuse to come.

"What was I supposed to do then? Go and get her, and take her away by force? I had the law on my side—I had documents. I had legal permission. But what am I supposed to do? Carry my own daughter, screaming that she doesn't want to go, away from her mother's house? I can't possibly do that, and I'm sure you can see why not!"

He shakes his head sadly.

"All the courts in the world couldn't make my little girl want to come and see me—and at that time, she was spending six-and-a-half days with her mom already. She wouldn't even spend one afternoon a week with me, not even one afternoon a week…"

Other noncustodial fathers tell similar stories.

"My kids would cry when I picked them up, at first," says one young father, wrinkling his face at the memory. "They were little at the time. I guess maybe they thought I was taking them away from their mom permanently. It was pretty hard to pick those kids up, both of them crying, and put them in my car for a few hours of visitation. Gradually they would calm down, and things would go okay, but next time it would be the same scene, all over again, more crying as we left their mom's house."

Life as a noncustodial parent is filled with angst—first at being separated from your own children for so much of the time, then for the lack of enthusiasm those children may show at "having to" spend time with you for a few hours during an evening or on a weekend.

As we've worked with separated and divorced couples over the past several decades, we've developed a fourfold line of approach we use to help noncustodial parents have the best experience possible as they struggle to adjust to the reality of being away from their children for long periods of time.

1. Communicate, Communicate, and Communicate

One of the greatest challenges faced by noncustodial parents is the great difficulty of maintaining a relationship—intermittently. Whether your visitation rights are frequent or infrequent, the simple fact remains that your children spend most of their time in someone else's home, bonding with another parent or another household and family unit.

Your best response to that is, *communicate.* In this area of easy Internet access, sending e-mail messages to your kids is an excellent way to stay in touch. One busy father we know, who is the noncustodial parent of two teens, IM's both of them every evening sometime between 9 PM and 10 PM. It's an arrangement known only to the three of them, as far as the father knows.

"They know I'll be online at that time, and I make absolutely sure that I'm logged on and available, every night of the week, 9 PM to 10 PM," the father relates. "I don't always have much to say—they don't always have much to say. But the point is, we talk to each other every night.

"Thank God for instant messaging—and I mean that literally! I couldn't afford the phone bill to talk to them, and their phone calls probably aren't private anyway, not in that house. But they can go online and talk to me, and they know I'll always be there for them, every night, just like usual.

"I have a better relationship with them now than I've ever had, and most of that has grown out of IM'ing," says the dad. "Don't get me wrong—I still wish I had them all the time. But I'm gradually adjusting to reality—that just isn't going to happen, at least not during their childhood. So right now I've got the next best thing: I 'talk' to my kids every single night."

Many noncustodial parents may not have access to current technology, or they may have children who are too young to be online late at night. In these cases, a frequent phone call can be just as positive.

"I'd call every night if I could," says one parent. "With my work schedule (self-employed) that isn't always possible. But I probably call at least three nights a week, sometimes more. I love hearing the sound of my kids' voices, even if they don't have much to say."

Sending a postcard or a personal note generally works, unless the parent with primary custody has a bad habit of intercepting the children's mail. One noncustodial father sent gift cards to his children for several months before discovering that they never actually reached the children. His ex-wife opened their mail, removed the cards, and sometimes threw his personal notes in the trash before his children even received them.

But however and whenever possible, noncustodial parents should communicate with their children. Keep in touch. Stay as informed as your children will let you be. Act interested but not "snoopy." Learn to ask open-ended questions, the kind that may lead to longer discussions and detailed answers.

2. Express Your Love Clearly and Often

For noncustodial parents, another challenge is maintaining the depth and quality of their relationships with their children. When funds are limited, and when opportunities to visit are few and far between, they can feel powerless—unable to fully express what's truly in their hearts.

"My kids measure love in time and money," sighs one father. "And guess what? I don't have either one of those. No wonder they don't like me very much."

Although this father's perception is probably inaccurate, his anxiety is familiar and common. Many noncustodial parents are living on very limited budgets. Sending extravagant gifts to their children is out of the question. For others, just coming for a visit exhausts available funds. There isn't enough money left over to do something "fun" during the visiting times.

What matters, counselors and therapists agree, is to express your love for your children clearly, consistently, appropriately, and often. If you don't have much money, you needn't pretend otherwise. If you can't come for a visit very often, don't raise your children's hopes by making promises you can't keep.

Instead, let your children know that you love them. Tell them so. Let them know you're proud of them, and be specific about the reasons why. Praise them for their accomplishments. Compliment them for things they're doing right. If you can't buy them something, make them something. Even if they don't use, wear, or particularly like the gift, you've still sent a message of affection and love, just by giving them a present.

Children are good at knowing when they're loved. Their inner receptors are remarkably good at spotting insincerity, inaccuracy, and phony concern. If your heart is full of love and affection for them, they'll probably realize that, but keep telling them so anyway. As the more "distant" parent, or at least the one with less access to their daily lives, go out of your way to be sure your kids hear you expressing your love for them.

"I know, Dad," they may sigh, rolling their eyes. Keep telling them anyway. Tell them until they've heard it so often it soaks deep down into their consciousness, down where they're probably still hurting over the loss of their original intact family unit. No matter what your family history has been, let your children know that your love for them is permanent and forever.

3. Make Very Few Promises, and Keep Them All

It's tempting, when wanting to impress your kids or manipulate them into liking you, to make extravagant promises about the future.

Whether it's "I'll buy you a new bicycle" or "I'll come back next week," your kids are listening. Although you may not express these thoughts as actual promises, kids tend to hear them that way.

When a new bicycle doesn't arrive, they are hurt and angry. When Dad does not return next week, they feel abandoned.

Be careful of how you speak. Stating good intentions may seem helpful to you, but it may have exactly the opposite effect on your children. By stating what you hope to do, or wish to be able to do, you are raising their expectations. Already hurting and stressed by the breakup of their family, kids are in no position to have their hopes dashed and their expectations lowered.

Broken promises—even if these statements weren't technically a commitment on your part—harm your children and weaken their respect for you. Kept promises—even small ones—have the opposite effect, happily.

"Unless I crash on the freeway, I'll be here next Sunday," one father often said to his young daughter.

"Don't talk like that, Daddy," she would often say.

Although he eventually changed his wording so his daughter wouldn't be afraid of losing him in a car accident, he was trying to communicate a simple truth: Unless some kind of major catastrophe occurs, we'll be together again in the very near future—for sure.

The daughter got the message. Her father was making a promise that nothing—at least nothing short of a really big problem—could keep them apart.

Making and keeping promises places a security blanket around the frightened edges of your children's hearts. Even if you can't be with them on a daily basis, you can establish a reassuring truth about yourself: When you say something, you mean it. When you promise something, you deliver it.

There may be no more effective way for a noncustodial parent to gain the trust and respect of his or her children than to make few promises—carefully—and then keep them, without exception.

Children notice when we follow through and honor them as we said we would. Children notice when we love them and keep our word.

4. Cooperate with the Custodial Parent, Even If It Kills You

We often phrase the point as above, simply for effect.

Many noncustodial parents, as much as they dearly love their children, greatly prefer to avoid all contact with their ex-partner. Maybe the wounds are still too fresh. Maybe the issue is resentment of that partner for having the blessing and privilege of primary custody.

No one is asking you to take your ex-partner to dinner, buy them a

gift, or otherwise shower them with affection. However, simple cour-
tesy and common decency go a long way to smoothing the relationships. It's often the little things: being on time for your appointments.
Being on time again when you return the kids. Getting the details right.
Remembering if there are medicines to administer, errands to run, things
or people to be picked up.

Every time you perform responsibly in your dealings with your
ex-spouse, you are sending a message of respect and cooperation.
Conversely, every time you are late, forgetful, or uncooperative, you
demonstrate a lack of respect your ex-partner will surely notice.

As much as you may want some sort of "revenge" on your ex-partner,
think carefully before using delay tactics, feigning forgetfulness, or otherwise taking out your frustration on your former spouse. After all, do you
really want to alienate the person who provides the primary care of your
children? Or would you rather be on good terms with that gatekeeper, so
access to your children is more easily and more often granted?

Be a diplomat. If foreign governments and sworn enemies can
figure out how to have dinner parties and be kind to each other in the
same small space, surely you can be civil and cooperative with your
ex-partner.

If you can do so successfully, your children will gain. They'll have access
to both parents, not just to one. You will gain—you'll have simpler and
pleasanter times with your children. And your ex-partner will gain—he or
she will feel respected by you and will respect you more fully in return.

Tips for Noncustodial Parents

Since your time with your children may be limited, it's wise to think carefully about your reputation with them. Here's a quick review of some of the best ideas for increasing your influence with your kids, even if you don't have the time, money, and access you so deeply wish to share with them.

1. *Communicate, communicate, communicate.* If you have access to newer technology, such as sending instant messages online or text messages on cell phones, do so. If your children are younger or if technology is limited, call when you can. Send cards, notes, and letters. Postcard stamps are cheap. Give them visible evidence you care about them—communicate!

2. *Express your love clearly and often.* Noncustodial parents sometimes want to "fix" their children and correct bad behaviors during their brief times together. While this may be an appropriate parental role, be sure that you show your love to your children. Be proud of them and say so. Compliment them often and specifically. Let your love show clearly, loudly, appropriately, and often. Speak up and praise your kids.

3. *Make very few promises, and keep them all.* Your children are listening to you. Don't raise their hopes by talking about your good intentions and wishes. They may hear these things as "promises" even if you don't intend it. Be very careful about making promises—and when you make a promise, move heaven and earth to keep your word. Your kids will notice if you are reliable, and their respect for you will increase.

4. *Be kind to the custodial parent, the "gatekeeper."* Show respect to your ex-partner by being on time, returning the kids to the agreed location, remembering medicines and their appointments, and by just generally being responsible. Speak positively and cooperatively to and about your ex-spouse. Everyone wins when you treat each other with respect. As the noncustodial parent, you have the most to gain—or lose.

Chapter Seven

Welcome to My Stress: Parenting Adolescents and Teens

THE ANGER AND PAIN OF THE ADOLESCENT YEARS OFTEN INTENSIFIES AS A RESPONSE TO DIVORCE

My mom's new boyfriend is really sweet!
He took me shopping last weekend and bought me
a lot of new clothes. Jeff is way easier to be around
than my dad is. My dad is always angry about something.
—Brittany, age 13, child of divorce

Brent and Lisa had one child, a daughter, during their decade of marriage. They divorced just before Madelyn's ninth birthday.

"We shared custody, and it worked pretty well," is how Brent recalls the early years of their divorce. "I had Madelyn one week. Lisa had her the next. Fridays were our days to trade back and forth. Both of us lived within driving distance of Maddie's school, so that wasn't an issue."

Neither Brent nor Lisa remarried at first. Both of them were careful about keeping their "romantic interests" away from the young daughter they shared. "I think Lisa was probably dating, and sometimes I was," Brent admits. "But I also think both of us tried to hide our partners from Madelyn as much as possible. I tended to do my 'socializing' during the weeks that I didn't have custody. As far as I know, Lisa was careful that way too."

In some ways, the divorce worked better than the marriage had. Major disagreements were rare. Both Brent and Lisa were employed in good jobs; somehow they avoided the typical fights over money or child support.

"I paid my dues, plus I gave a lot more above that," Brent reports. "Neither of us wanted to be stingy with our daughter. We wanted her to have the best life we could give her, especially since we'd split up her family."

Things were reasonably smooth until Madelyn began the transition into adolescence. Suddenly his daughter didn't want to be around him anymore. He was confused and disappointed.

"I didn't notice the pattern at first," Brent recalls. "Madelyn was always giving me valid excuses why she couldn't come over—a cheerleading clinic, some 'away' games she had to cheer for. There was always a good reason for not being able to see me. She was so nice about it, I didn't notice at first she had basically quit coming to my house."

When he did recognize the trend, he confronted his daughter. It's a choice he still regrets making.

"She just blew up at me!" he exclaims, sighing. "She started yelling and telling me that her reasons (for not coming over) were completely personal. Then she started talking about how hard it was to switch back and forth, back and forth, all the time. I could tell she was defensive; I couldn't figure out what I had said or done that triggered such a huge emotional blowup! She was angry, and she stayed that way. Our conversation ended badly.

"Not only that, about a day later Lisa called me, all upset, and yelled at me for being mean to our daughter. I guess Madelyn had talked to her about it, so now both of them were mad at me."

Brent knew he'd blown it, but he didn't know what he'd done wrong. "I was seeing a counselor anyway for some other stuff," he explains, "so I decided to use some of my counseling time to explore this whole thing of Madelyn not wanting to stay at my house anymore."

The counselor pointed Brent in helpful directions.

He let a few weeks pass, then invited his daughter to dinner—not at his house, but at her choice of restaurant. He spent most of the meal listening, not talking—not trying to push the conversation around to his own personal agenda. Finally, late in the meal, after they had laughed together and were somewhat relaxed, he raised some questions.

"This time, Madelyn wasn't defensive," Brent remembers. "This time she trusted me and trusted my motives. Or maybe I just caught her on a good day."

What Brent learned was that his teen daughter "just didn't feel comfortable" at his house anymore. She couldn't, or didn't, explain what she meant. Brent returned to the counselor with that information, hoping for some useful answers.

> **"I left like I'd lost her for good,
> like I was no longer important in her life."**

The counselor helped Brent unravel some of the mysteries. "While I was at work, Madelyn sometimes wandered around and looked through all my stuff. She would sometimes find women's clothes or personal things, so she'd know that someone had been 'visiting' me. She would sometimes find men's magazines—nothing really bad, just man stuff—and that bothered her. I guess the combination of those things made my house somehow less comfortable for her, made her want to spend a lot less time there. She started asking me if she could live at her mom's house permanently."

In Brent and Lisa's case, though a court had declared joint custody and though both parents were in agreement, none of that mattered. Madelyn, by her own choice, simply ignored the custody arrangement and decided she'd stay with her mom most of the time.

Visits with her father became few and increasingly far between. Brent was devastated.

"Especially for her last two years of high school, I was bummed about 'losing' my daughter," he recalls. "I felt like I'd lost her for good, like I was no longer important in her life. I got depressed easily, and I stayed depressed for long periods of time."

What changed, if anything?

"Nothing at all, until Madelyn went to college," Brent explains. "Somehow that was the beginning of a new relationship with her. In fact, when she'd come home from college, she began to choose coming home to my house, instead of her mom's.

"Her mother got sort of jealous of that—but what could she say? After all, she'd had most of Maddie's high school years all to herself. Finally, now that Madelyn was mostly grown up, it seemed like it was becoming my turn to be the primary parent. Whatever was happening, I was glad about that."

Brent was hugely curious about his daughter's change in preferences. By asking good questions and listening quietly to the answers, he later learned at least part of what was causing Madelyn to alter her habits.

"Every time I go home (to Mom's)," Madelyn sighed late one Saturday night during a weekend visit, "she asks me all kinds of questions about guys, about relationships, about my personal life. I get so tired of being interrogated all the time. I just hate that!"

By contrast, it was obvious that her father's laid-back, accepting style, not asking the prying questions, made an impact on his university-age daughter. Brent "won back" the heart of his daughter by simply accepting her, being grateful for their time together, and not bothering her about her sex life and dating habits.

Although he was greatly curious—especially about her "social life" and arrangements with men—Brent quickly realized that by waiting for Madelyn to open up and reveal herself, he would learn more than if he pressured her with intense questions and detailed probing.

A recipe for others to follow? Perhaps in some situations, while coping with the changes and stresses that are normal in dealing with adolescents and teens.

Fight or Flight

Adolescent and family counselors tend to agree that "backing off" can be an effective strategy with older teens and college-age sons and daughters. As they begin to build a valid and useful sense of independence from their parents, it's typical and expected for older teens to resent parents' questions and rebel against their attempts at control. As these increasingly independent persons learn by choosing and by experience, parents may do best to pray and wait, staying available to be consulted as counselors or advisors.

Meanwhile, with younger teens, backing off may send entirely the wrong message. With younger teens, family counselors insist, there can

be a constant exploring of limits and boundaries—with the teens themselves hoping to find that the boundaries are firmly in place. Even if they
test the limits and complain a lot about the rules, younger teens tend
to find security within well-defined limits about family and personal
behavior.

These patterns do not merely hold within a divorce setting, they
may intensify and move toward the extreme. An adolescent who is
"exploring" anyway may end up going "further out there" as an angry
or confused response to the breakup of his or her family. A teen that
is already sullen and withdrawn, rarely communicating with other
members of her family, may go into a fully silent mode, choosing not
to talk with anyone at all.

Not uncommonly, some teens find refuge in spending all their time
asleep. Concerned custodial parents, worried that something is wrong
with their children, confront family counselors with news of their child's
sleep habits—coming home from school, grabbing a snack, then going
to bed.

"She goes straight to bed when she gets home from school, gets up
for dinner—or doesn't, it varies—then goes back to sleep," one divorced
mom complained to the counselor. "What's wrong with my daughter?"

While many parents would gladly accept a "problem" such as their
teen choosing to sleep too much, parents who experience this phenomenon can be greatly worried and anxious.

Such parents needn't always worry. Choosing to sleep through the
late afternoon and evening is a fairly common response to a stressful
season in life—such as the aftermath of a divorce or the transition to a
new school or a new social setting—which challenges or frightens the
teen. As a way of simply not dealing with a scary reality, some teens
choose to sleep.

With the help of a family counselor, one divorced mom moved from anxiety and stress to gratefully accepting her daughter's sleep habits. The counselor helped the worried mother realize several things: 1) her daughter was safely at home, 2) her daughter's eating habits seemed normal, and 3) her daughter was sleeping alone (not with a partner).

"It still doesn't seem right!" the mother insisted. However, waiting and watching, the mom saw her daughter—after nearly an entire school year of sleeping all the time—gradually return to her prior habits and a more normal sleep cycle. The return to typical patterns was an outward symptom that she was making the necessary inner adjustments to the stresses and challenges of life.

Children and teens who experience the breakup of their family may respond in many different ways, acting out their fear, anger, and stress in a manner that fits their own personality and temperament. While there may be behaviors and patterns that need to be confronted, there may also be times when the parent simply needs to back away, pray, and wait.

In Brent's case, the challenge of losing Madelyn caused him to be all the more grateful when she finally returned to a deeper, more satisfying relationship with him. Though he felt like he had missed the best years of his daughter's life, he discovered instead that he shared with her the choices, challenges, and decisions that framed her entry into adulthood.

Although it's not a trade-off he consciously made, Brent is grateful that he didn't end up losing his daughter's affection permanently. Rather, by remaining available, he became her preferred counselor later in life.

Would Brent have advice for other divorced dads who might be experiencing a similar sense of estrangement or separation from their teen daughters?

"Well, cleaning up your act wouldn't hurt," he admits. "I should have realized that having those magazines around was not a positive thing.

And when I entertained women at my house, I should have realized Madelyn might find some of their stuff.

"I wish I would have handled things differently when Madelyn was younger, because I really lost out on a few years of her life there. I'm just glad she came back later, even deciding she preferred my house to her mom's. Today we have a really positive, solid, healthy relationship. I'm almost not even her father anymore, I'm really more of a peer."

Building a Relationship for the Future

Kerry, a committed Christian and churchgoer, was divorced by her husband after 14 years and three children together. She was awarded primary custody by the courts, which her husband did not contest.

Within a few months, the pattern of parenting looked like this: Kerry was the rule-maker, the boundary-setter, the parent who struggled to make ends meet financially. Her ex-husband was the generous guy, the big spender, the one whose motto seemed to be "Party, party, party" when he had the kids for a weekend or for a special trip.

"I was so jealous of him, and so mad at him," Kerry admits. "He was basically buying the kids' affection, and it worked! They always loved being with their dad—and who wouldn't? He was 'Mr. Fun Guy' to them."

Meanwhile, it was Mom who constantly made the rules, monitored the rules, and enforced the rules. If Dad was "all fun," then Mom felt like "no fun" much of the time. Yet she was unwilling to abandon her children to the kind of no-discipline, no-boundaries approach her ex-husband seemed to favor.

As her children began to reach their teen years, Kerry's parenting style started to change. For one thing, she found she simply didn't have the energy to chase three children—teens and preteens—around the house all day, checking to be sure each one was behaving properly. She worked, came home exhausted at times, and was also getting older—

a combination that caused her to feel tired, depleted, and worn out on many evenings.

Without reading a book on parenting teens, and without seeing a counselor for sage advice, Kerry emerged into a different style of parenting just as her children were emerging into their adolescent years. It was a blessed serendipity of exhaustion and life stage: a confluence of a mother's lost energy and the rising energy levels of three active, noisy teens and preteens.

"I just couldn't find that much time anymore," says Kerry, interpreting the changes she made and the reasons for those changes. "I didn't have the energy to play policeman to three highly active kids (by that time ages 15, 12, and 10). I didn't really make a conscious decision—instead I found myself kind of guarding my own energy and my own emotional health. I had to—if I didn't take care of me, nobody else was going to do it!"

Kerry's accidental or divinely inspired discovery highlights a wise approach to parenting teens, especially for divorced mothers and fathers. She began making the transition from a supervisory, authority-type figure—appropriate and useful for younger children—to a caring, interested adult who saved her "fighting energy" for the times that most required it.

"I was absolutely shocked when my daughter and I finally became friends," Kerry remembers. "We had fought so much, when she was younger. When Kayla was maybe 12 or 13, I think we fought for one whole year. All we did was fight! It seemed like all I ever did was yell at her, and she'd yell right back at me. I think she hated me—she said she did—but I wasn't ready to change the rules or quit caring about her life."

Kerry is pensive for a moment. "Whether it was me changing my style, or her growing up—somehow we emerged into close friends, just when I least expected it. And it wasn't because I quit caring about her or quit enforcing boundaries. It was because I started backing away from the small stuff and only getting involved when a major issue was on the line.

"I didn't have the strength to let everything become a major issue!"

Choosing Your Battles Carefully

While no one is suggesting that adolescents should be given few or no boundaries about acceptable behavior, busy divorced parents are well served by deciding, carefully and for themselves, what their real priorities will be. These may vary with each teen, according to the unique temperament, personality, and learning style of each.

"We actually did that in writing," says Angie, a divorced mom who remarried, sharing custody of her children with a new husband. "Jack and I would go out for breakfast on a Saturday morning, and we'd make little lists of what we were trying to achieve with each of the kids. By that time, we had one in high school and two in middle school. We didn't make those lists every Saturday obviously—it was probably something like three or four times a year. But several times a year we sat there over coffee and eggs, thinking about each child, deciding what kinds of changes we wanted to see and cause and help in each of our children."

Angie and Jack decided, for example, not to argue with any of their teens about clothing. While most parents may not be ready to abandon all input on the precarious subject of apparel and dress codes, this choice was liberating for Angie and Jack. With this one united decision, they saved themselves numerous battles at home.

"I didn't like how Angie's daughter was dressing," Jack admits. "To me, she looked like a tramp. She didn't have a promiscuous lifestyle, as far as we knew. But she wore clothes that made it look like she did— at least to her mom and me. But when we took a good hard look at the two or three most important areas where we wanted to see improvements for Becca, we both realized that changing her outward appearance didn't make our top three."

So what did the "top three list" look like at that stage of Becca's life?

"I might still have the list," Angie laughs. "I kept a lot of that stuff, even with coffee stains on some of the pages, because we've watched God work in some amazing ways on things from those lists."

Their top three list from this occasion contained the following goals for Angie's daughter Rebecca, age 16:

- higher self-image and self-esteem
- better grades in school
- at least one new close friend from the youth group

"We didn't show these lists to our kids," Angie says. "But we took these lists and used them to pray for the kids, and also to help us decide where our energy was really going to be directed, on a case-by-case, child-by-child basis. Having the lists helped us figure out where we really wanted to focus our prayers and our time and our energy."

Did they see success from any of the lists? Can they point to any?

"Well, since we're already talking about how Becca would dress," Angie mentions, "let's look at that one. As we said, it didn't even make our list for her; we decided we had some higher priorities.

"About six months after we focused our prayers on Becca's self-image, her grades, and at least one new close friend at church, she transformed her whole 'look'—and we hadn't pressured her or yelled at her about that, not even once.

"What happened was that she did develop some new friends in the youth group, and gradually she started looking more like they did and dressing more like they did. There were two girls in particular: both of them dressed more modestly than Becca did, at that stage. I don't know if they talked to her or if anything was said. I just know Becca gradually changed her look. The clothes we used to worry about so much, when she walked out of the house—she gave all that stuff away."

Jack interjects with a comment. "That's not exactly success from our lists," he smiles. "After all, that wasn't even on our list for Becca!"

Angie agrees. "You're right," she tells Jack. "But don't you think maybe God's answer to our prayers for a friend at church, and God's answers to our prayers for higher self-esteem in Becca, may have helped change the way she dressed?"

"Good point," Jack concurs. "And I'm also glad I didn't yell at her during those years. I couldn't stand the way she dressed—it reminded me of the 'working girls' I would see during my days in the military. I was really angry about having a new daughter who dressed that way, but God and Angie kept me from expressing that anger the way I would have. Instead of yelling at her about it, Angie and I started praying about things that were more important. And for whatever reason—we can't take the credit, and we don't know how it happened—Becca changed her look."

Jack looks down at his feet. "If I had yelled at her, she might have just kept on dressing like that. It might have backfired on me. I hadn't ever been the father of a teen daughter before, and it's not like I was very good at it."

Angie sees it differently. "Jack was steady and stable. Our kids knew they could count on him. After their dad's craziness and unpredictability, what Jack brought to our family was calmness. Jack is a rock—our kids needed something like that, especially right then."

By choosing their battles carefully, and by focusing on the most important goals they had for each child, Jack and Angie were able to watch as God brought positive changes into the lives of their growing teens.

"Not everything changed," Angie sighs. "We didn't see automatic or quick changes to anything. It wasn't like that. But we did watch God at work. And we did see many of the things on our list actually happen."

"God is good," Jack says succinctly.

Intercession: Unlocking God's Power Through Prayer

In some ways, watching God accomplish change in your teens is much like watching God make changes in the life of an adult you know at work or within your larger family circle. Since you are not in control of that adult, your options do not include supervising, managing, and enforcing changes in the actions, thoughts, behaviors, and choices of the other person.

Given that reality, what option is left?

Highest on your list should be prayer. As you pray for other adults, God works in at least two spheres of influence: your own heart, and the heart and life of the other person. God chooses to change the world, and human hearts, by means of the power of prayer.

Praying for your teens—consistently, specifically, directed toward goals you've set or realized—may be the single most powerful thing you can do if your goal is to watch transformation take place. Prayer releases the supernatural power of God to graciously invade the attention and life of another person.

> As you focus your efforts and your energies on intercessory prayer, you will have a front-row seat in the theater of God's transforming grace.

While prayer is neither a "quick fix" nor an "automatic answer," it does begin to transform your own thoughts and opinions about those you pray for. If you are angry at your teens, frustrated by their lack of response, or annoyed by their frequent acts of rebellion, you may find your heart softening toward them as you pray, night by night or morning by morning, for each of them.

If you are depressed about how your teens behave and feel like you have failed them as a father or mother; if you wonder if divorce has ruined them forever; you may find a surprising optimism emerging within your own heart as you pray. God is slow to give up on people—slow to abandon someone and move on. You may begin to watch gradual but certain transformation in the character and values of your children. You may also notice the same transformations within yourself.

If you are remarried, or if you have access to a close spiritual friend, make the time to pray together, adult with adult, for the needs of your children. Doing so with another parent will allow you to pray for each person's children in clear, specific, tangible ways—inviting God to work visibly and directly in their lives.

Fortunately for all of us, including divorced parents of teens, God delights in hearing and answering the prayers of His children. As you focus your efforts and your energies on intercessory prayer, you will have a front-row seat in the theater of God's transforming grace. Whether swiftly or slowly, whether all at once or over a long period of time, you will watch as God answers your prayers, sometimes in surprising and dramatic ways.

If you can give only one gift to the teens in your life, give them the gift of a praying parent. A mom who intercedes—a dad who prays—can make all the difference as a child navigates the challenging waters of adolescence.

Holding On or Letting Go:
Tips for Parents of Adolescents

Keep in mind that being the mom or dad of an emerging teen will probably raise your blood pressure a few points! You'll have ample opportunity to experience frustration, disappointment, and resentment—and your teens will be experiencing the same things.

At Younger Ages, Boundaries Matter

Pre-teens and younger teens are well served by having established boundaries. When a parent suddenly becomes lax or quits caring about the rules, this confuses and disorients a teen just as he or she is struggling to find appropriate independence.

Set clear standards for behavior, communicate your values consistently, and monitor your younger teen's whereabouts, friendships, and online patterns. You'll be helping him or her by staying involved and by maintaining your standards. Even if your teen complains, experts agree that he or she will be grateful to encounter those boundaries.

With Older Youth, Back Off While Still Caring

Older teens are en route to adulthood. Many of them will need to learn through their own experiences, including experiences that you'd greatly prefer they avoid. Realize that you can't possibly monitor or control every aspect of an older teen's behavior—especially once he or she has a driver's license, works at a steady job, or goes off to college.

This doesn't mean changing your values! You can continue to communicate your own beliefs, values, and hopes. If you made mistakes when you were their age, this may be a good time to admit those to your older teen, explaining where and how you went wrong and what the consequences were. Be vulnerable and open, not "preachy."

Older teens will be watching how you actually live much more than listening to what you recommend. If you live a sexually active lifestyle—if you drink alcohol in social settings and to relax—you can expect your older teen to follow your example rather than listening to your advice. Older teens are watching for consistency. When a parent sends one message but lives another, they notice the difference.

Choose your fights carefully. Instead of arguing with older teens about their taste in music, clothing, entertainment, and so on, allow them more freedom in these areas as they become older. Make as few rules as possible, but enforce those rules clearly and consistently—otherwise, your boundaries are meaningless.

Save your energy for the things that matter most: learn to overlook the less-important issues so that you can invest your strength where it's most needed.

Let Birth Parents Set Boundaries and Enforce Rules

When a divorced person remarries, he or she may be hoping to gain some help with the difficult task of parenting. Particularly if a woman has been single for a while, she may be hoping that having "a man in the house" will cause her children or teens to behave better or show more respect.

Experience confirms that older children and teens are often highly resistant to new authority figures in their lives. Regardless of the marital status and life experiences of their birth parents, children of all ages may harbor the secret hope that their birth parents will re-unite and re-form the original family. Stepparents, especially those who try too hard to assert control or build a relational bond, may find their best efforts resisted and opposed by their partner's children.

In the early days of a remarriage, it's usually wisest to let the birth parent continue to set, monitor, and enforce the boundaries for children of all ages. This allows older children and teens the chance to adjust to the presence of a new adult in their lives—and to readjust their expectations about the family they now live in.

Stepparents can be very useful and can successfully exercise leadership within a newly forming family. However, slow and steady wins the race. Trying too hard, coming on too strong, making too many changes—these and other tactics can backfire, causing problems as the family attempts to unify and grow strong.

If you are a birth parent who is getting remarried, expect to continue your present load of parenting duties, at least for a while. Gradually allow your new partner to witness, participate in, and eventually suggest changes to the parenting style in your home. Doing it in this way allows your children the time and space they need to adjust to a new parent.

Pray Without Ceasing!

As our children grow into youth and adulthood, our relationship with them changes. Our responsibility to them changes also. We are no longer able to monitor their behavior and control their choices. Instead, we are uniquely qualified to guide them by providing wise counsel, thoughtful insights from our own experiences, and above all, constant prayer.

Praying for your adolescents and teens releases God's power into their lives and also into yours. As you daily intercede for them, you may find your love for them increasing. As you listen to their searching questions and even to their petty grievances, you may find yourself identifying more closely with their perspective.

Today's adolescents especially need our prayers. The world in which they are coming of age presents radically new choices and opportunities to them, often without giving them an appropriate moral or value-related context. As you pray for God's protection around them—as you pray about the peer relationships they form—you may find yourself closer to a loving God than ever before.

You may also learn, perhaps for the first time, how deeply and consistently God loves *you*—even when your own choices are harmful or unwise.

PART THREE

For Better or Worse—
To Remarry or Remain Alone

CHAPTER EIGHT

Flying Solo:
Why You Might Consider It

LOOKING BACK WITH GRATITUDE,
BUT ALSO WITH SOME REGRETS

*The idea that God is actively nurturing us,
so that we might grow up to be like Him,
brings us face to face with our own laziness.*
—M. Scott Peck

Now that your divorce is final, should you consider getting married for a second time? If so, how will your choice affect your children? If you choose to consider remarrying, how long should you wait before dating again?

In the next two chapters, we'll explore four life stories that highlight the choices and challenges involved in choosing to remain single or in deciding to marry a new partner. Later on, in our "roundtable" chapter

(chapter 11), we'll learn together from the experiences of four divorced people—three women, one man—who carefully and prayerfully made their own choices about marrying again or staying single. We'll also learn their perspectives on healing and recovery.

In this chapter, we'll explore "flying solo"—that is, making a choice to remain single, perhaps while sharing custody of your children with an ex-partner and that person's new spouse. As you'll see from what follows, no decision is simple. No option results in a "perfect solution" to the many challenges you face.

Debbie's Story: Two Sons, No Husband "Did I Do the Right Thing?"

Debbie welcomes us to her office. Bright, well-dressed, and in her 40s, she has recently been promoted to management level—she's a senior loan officer at a community credit union near a large military base.

"This is my lunch break," she says, smiling as we enter her office. "So don't worry, I'm not wasting my employer's time by talking to you!"

We smile and relax. This is our first meeting with Debbie; we will meet with her two more times in order to listen carefully to her story and learn from her experiences. The next two meetings will happen in her home and in a nearby coffee shop that she visits most mornings on the drive to work.

"This (last) weekend, I had my first date in more than 15 years," she begins as we settle into comfortable stuffed armchairs. "It feels strange. I'm really glad I didn't try this before now. I don't think I could have handled it!"

We've been seeking interviews with people who chose to "fly solo," and several women we know have pointed us in Debbie's direction. We've not met her until this interview, although we share mutual friends and acquaintances.

"She's really been wise about everything," says a divorced friend.

"Of all the people I know, she's been the smartest in handling her kids, her career, and everything else," a woman at her church says of her. "She's been a role model for all of us single parents."

"A role model?" Debbie asks in disbelief as we begin our interview by mentioning the comments. "I don't think I'm a role model for anything. What I am is…"—she searches for words for a minute—"I am a survivor. So if you want to call me something, call me that—a survivor."

As we learn throughout our three interviews with her, Debbie is much more than simply a survivor. She's raised two sons, essentially alone. She's learned a new job skill, then pursued further education to advance in her chosen career. She's not only stayed involved at her local church, she's led small groups and served as a devotional speaker for several women's meetings. Looking in from the outside, you'd think she was successful, content, and fulfilled—she makes the divorced life look smooth and manageable.

You'd be surprised to learn how Debbie sees it. "I'm still wondering if I've made the right choices," she admits early in our first interview. "I was lucky enough to have several men seem interested in me right after the divorce, but it was too early for me. I couldn't think about men, and I didn't even remotely want to think about dating!"

In the three or four years immediately after the divorce, years of financial and emotional struggle and constant painful adjustments, she made the choice to stay single—at least as long as her boys were living at home.

"I didn't really consult them about it," she recalls. "They were seven and five when the whole divorce thing blew up in our faces. It caught me by surprise, and it absolutely blew them away.

"They hadn't seen or heard us fighting very much—we rarely fought at all—so they had no idea their family might be breaking apart. And to tell you the truth, I was pretty much a basket case, especially at first. I cried myself to sleep at night, and I cried during the day after I got my boys off to school. I would sit at home, make myself some coffee, and just cry."

Walter, Debbie's husband of nearly ten years, the father of her two young sons, got involved with a woman at work and chose to leave his family for her. Within a month or so of walking away from his family, he made a second announcement: His girlfriend was pregnant.

"I didn't know how to explain *that* to my boys," she sighs. "They were way below the age of explaining those issues. I remember my younger son kind of looking at me, then asking, 'So, is Daddy going to start a whole new family?'"

Essentially, the answer to that question was "yes."

Debbie did not contest the divorce, so the process was fairly simple. The young couple's assets were few; their debts were many. "The hardest part about the whole divorce was figuring out who would keep what loans and obligations," she remembers. "We didn't fight over that—I was in shock, unable to really fight at that time—but it was sort of hard to break up the debts between us."

Was that struggle the source of Debbie's new occupation?

"Maybe," Debbie muses aloud. "Most of all I felt helpless in a financial sense. I hadn't worked outside the home during our marriage, except some part-time and seasonal jobs. I devoted myself entirely to raising my boys and keeping our household in good order. I enjoyed being a stay-at-home mom!"

Until the day her entire world crumbled apart beneath her.

"Walter just walked away," is how Debbie remembers it. "He talked to us for a minute around the breakfast table, then he literally just walked out of the house. I found out later he had been moving some of his clothes and things—very gradually—into an apartment with his girlfriend."

It was a week or so before he came back, on a school day while the boys were in class, to complete his move and retrieve the rest of "his" things.

"At that time, I didn't even know what was happening to me yet." Debbie shrugs. "I was still trying to process what was going on here. I couldn't understand it! The next thing I know, Walter is at the door, along with this young girl in shorts, and the two of them are carrying stuff out of my house and putting it in the back of a rental truck."

What did she do about it?

She hesitates for a minute before replying. "I just went into the boys' room, closed the door, sat down on Robert's bunk bed, and cried," Debbie tells us in a voice softened to a gentle whisper. "I felt weak. I was angry, I was afraid, and I was in a complete state of shock. I guess I kind of thought that Walter and his girlfriend wouldn't be taking anything from my sons' room."

Eventually she heard the truck start up and drive away.

"He took my college stereo system!" Debbie exclaims in wonder. "But I got that back in the settlement. By the time we got around to dividing things up, I was starting to realize I needed to pay attention. I needed to stand up for myself, because no one else was going to."

For a long time after the divorce became final, she kept the paperwork on the top of a dresser in her bedroom. "I would pick up the papers, look at them, put them back down," she remembers. "Somehow all that paperwork was my only connection with my previous life as a happy wife. I would pick up those papers and not really read them, but just kind of stare at them for a while."

It took several years for Debbie to decide to remain single. "As I started to say, I didn't really consult with my boys about that," she confesses. "By then they were getting adjusted to bouncing back and forth between their dad's house—where they had a cute little baby sister to play with—and the apartment I moved into after the divorce."

What were the main factors driving her choice to stay single?

"I remember thinking that if I dated and got married, it would just confuse the boys even more," she says. "It seemed like things would be simpler if I kept something—our little family unit—as safe and unchanged as possible. I don't think I made some big, conscious decision—although I did spend a lot of time thinking and praying about it. It was more like I just kind of grew in that direction. I kept thinking that 'less change is better' for the boys. And to be really honest with you, I was kind of burned out on men at that moment in my life," she remarks candidly.

Were there times that she doubted the wisdom of her choice?

"Only every day!" Debbie replies, laughing. "Including today, and now my sons are grown adults who don't live at home anymore. I'm not ready to give advice to anyone, certainly not a divorced woman, about whether or not she should get remarried. I know *I* couldn't have handled the pressures of dating and relationships, plus raising my sons alone. It was too much!

"But I still wonder if I did the right thing by staying single. When my sons were in their teen years and our relationship wasn't so good, I would wonder if having a man around the house would be helpful to them. I couldn't be the dad they needed, and their real father was busy reliving his own childhood."

How did she survive those years when her sons were being normal rebellious teens, not wanting to be so "close" to their mother?

"It was hard for me, which is an understatement," Debbie says. "My boys were the only thing I hung onto, and during their teen years they were busy trying *not* to be so close to me. I did my share of crying during those years, and I yelled at them too much. It seems like I was always yelling at them about something."

Did her friends understand her choices during those years?

"Oh my goodness," she recalls. "Everyone I knew was trying to fix me up with someone. Everybody was being so 'helpful' all the time. I couldn't move or breathe or go to church, even, without someone telling me about this guy they thought would be just perfect for me. In a weird way, it was almost easier to disappoint *everybody* than to take one person's suggestion and ignore the rest. I just kept saying, 'No, thanks.'"

In our final interview with Debbie, we ask her to explain how she views the advantages and the disadvantages of the choice she made to remain single while raising her two young sons.

"I probably see the disadvantages more than most people do," she begins, "so let's start there if we can. Here are few of those, in random order.

"My sons went through their teen years without a dad in their home. They visited their father, but when they did they were in a very non-Christian house and environment. Their dad has HBO and SHO and every other movie channel. He drinks a lot. I'm sorry to sound so judgmental, but their dad's house is just a very different place than my home.

> "There was just me. That simple fact drove me to my knees a lot, trusting God and praying. My faith in God got a lot stronger as I watched Him work miracles for us."

"I was lonely a lot of the time, especially as the boys got older. When they were young, they were my whole life. Then as they got older...I didn't have a life. I spent a lot of time trapped between being lonely, which I was, yet not wanting to confuse my life and my family with dating, relationships, and all that pressure.

"I might have been a more balanced person with a partner at my side. Having a godly man right there in the kitchen might have helped me mature faster or grow up more quickly. I don't know...We probably would have had more money too, especially in those first five or six years. I really struggled just to pay rent. My car broke down all the time, and we survived that only because of some helpful men at church. They have a whole ministry of car repair—and I think I've been their main customer."

Debbie seems finished with the disadvantages, so we gently remind her we're interested in what she sees as the plus side of staying single.

She is thoughtful in answering this question. "Well, for one thing, I probably relied on God a lot more," she acknowledges. "What I wanted, especially in my lonely times, was someone else to carry the load, someone else to take the responsibility, someone else to make all the tough decisions and choices. But there wasn't anybody else. There was just me. That simple fact drove me to my knees a lot, trusting God and praying. My faith in God got a lot stronger as I watched Him work miracles for us."

We interrupt to ask about the miracles.

"Well, just little things really," she says, remembering. "We would have a financial crisis or something, and at the last minute someone would send me a little note with a check in it, and that amount of money would be exactly what we needed to pay the rent. I should have kept a journal of those things. It happened a lot—never a large sum of money—I didn't win the lottery or anything—but somehow when we would have a need, God would supply it in small but amazing ways.

"I'm certain my relationship with God today is a lot stronger, and a lot deeper, and a lot more genuine, than if I was still married to Walter," Debbie continues. "In my married years I was kind of coasting along, letting Walter be the leader. Then after he was gone, I wanted someone else to just take over his role, but I wasn't willing to go through all the hassle of dating. So I had to step up and be my own leader—and that made me rely on God for His wisdom.

"In the first few years after my divorce, years that were just enormously painful and frustrating and horrible, somehow my relationship with God grew deeper and stronger and closer. Being single kept me relying on God and focused on knowing Him. Probably the reason I do some devotional speaking now is that I actually have a devotional life and a prayer life now. Believe me, divorce is *great* for your prayer life!"

We ask Debbie how her sons feel about her choice to remain single while they were young. Has she ever asked them? Have they ever voluntarily shared their opinions with their mother?

She laughs. "My younger son left for college two years ago. Just before he left, he sat down with me in the living room for a 'serious talk.' I didn't know what he intended to say, he looked so serious. He said, 'Mom, John is already living on his own, and now I'm going away to school. You may not know it yet, but you're going to be awfully lonely once I'm not here! I think you really ought to get out there and start dating. Maybe you should look around at church and find some nice divorced guy...'"

Debbie laughs again in remembering. "It was the sweetest thing. My son was worrying about me, actually wanting me to date and have a relationship. And honestly, it was probably his advice that started me thinking about it, at least. Up until that time, I had kept the 'dating doors' completely shut, with everyone and at all times. Life was simpler without all that confusion."

Now, finally, she has had her first date.

"I already knew this guy," she says simply. "And we are already friends, we just hadn't complicated things by 'dating' before. So we are taking this whole thing very, very slowly. We talk about everything, all the time. We've had only one 'date' so far—and we both seemed to survive that okay. We talked about how weird it felt to be dating, but really we just got together as friends, like we always do. It didn't feel pressured or artificial—it felt nice. So we'll see what's ahead for me, but I'm not in a hurry."

Fifteen years after her divorce, two years after her younger child left home for college, Debbie is dating again. For her, staying single made sense while the children were at home. Their absence from the home brings her a sense of personal freedom now—in her 40s.

"I'm young!" Debbie smiles. "I could get married today and be together with my husband for 40 years, maybe more. So I feel like all the options are open to me—but like I said, I'm not in a hurry.

"I think God will show me what to do. He always has."

Jeremy's Choice: One Daughter, No Wife
"I Will Wait for Her"

Jeremy's wife left him for no apparent reason. So far as he could tell, there wasn't another person involved. His wife just walked away.

"She's had a couple of serious boyfriends in these ten years," he sighs, "but she's never gotten engaged. I assume she's sleeping with guys. But to my knowledge, there wasn't 'another man' when she left—she just wanted out of our marriage."

Jeremy looks down at his feet while he talks. He takes long, slow sips of double espresso throughout our conversation with him. He is slow to speak, lost in thought, definitely a "thinker."

"She left both of us," he says softly. "That's what really surprised me. We had a three-year-old daughter together, this beautiful baby girl, and my wife didn't just leave me—she left Marisa as well."

He was granted custody because his ex-wife wanted it that way. Without knowing it, he is part of an emerging minitrend in child custody; single custodial fathers are a growing segment of the twenty-first-century adult population in North America.

Jeremy is unconcerned with trends. "How could anyone possibly leave Marisa?" he wonders aloud. "Sure, she was noisy and hyperactive as a two-year-old. But by the time Grace left us, Marisa had grown out of that toddler-trouble stage. She was talkative and friendly, well-behaved and adorable. How can a person just walk away from their only child?"

Men are coping with the challenges of single parenting in ever-increasing numbers, struggling with child-raising and household-management issues while also working full-time outside the home. On a trail well-blazed by single mothers, single fathers now find themselves searching daily for their next steps. For Jeremy, it's already been a ten-year journey.

"Marisa is 13," he says, shaking his head as if this is impossible. "Now, more than ever, she really needs a mother in her life. She's going through changes I've never experienced, ones I can't really explain to her. I feel awkward around her almost all the time these days. I never felt that way while she was younger. Now all of a sudden, she's starting to grow up, and I'm really aware of how 'non-female' I am."

He is silent for a while.

We ask about his decision not to remarry—it's the reason we've chosen to interview him. His thoughtful answer is that he still feels married to his ex-wife even though their divorce has been final for many years. In Jeremy's view, a marriage is forever.

"I will wait for her," he says quietly but firmly. "I decided that on the day she left us. I think, as a Christian, my obligation to God and to Grace is to wait for her, to keep the option of 'returning' always open to her."

Would it matter if Grace remarried? Would that change how he views his role and his responsibility?

"Not at all," he asserts. "This isn't about what Grace chooses, and it isn't about whether she marries a guy or just lives with him. This is about an open door in my heart and my home—I want Grace to know my door will always be open to her, forever—as long as I'm alive."

We ask Jeremy how old he is.

"I'm 37," he says. "I was 26 when Grace left. It's been a little over ten years since then, and I am absolutely committed to waiting."

Jeremy has willingly consented to this interview, and we sense his permission to ask him some of the hard questions: How do you cope with being alone; how do you respond to people who want you to start dating again?

He smiles ruefully. "My friends have given up," he says with a wry grin. "It took them a while, but they finally believe me now. I will not—ever—remarry, as long as Grace is alive. My daughter knows that, my friends know that, everyone at my church knows that—and most importantly, Grace knows that."

It sounds like a lonely life, we muse aloud.

"I think all single people are lonely," Jeremy opines. "Including the ones that haven't ever been married. At least in my case, Grace and I had five years together—two before Marisa was born, and three after. A lot of people never receive the gift I had for five years, the gift of being in a marriage relationship with a loving partner. I know for sure that God didn't 'owe me' a marriage. I didn't receive this great gift of five years together because I was somehow a good person. I'm just a normal guy; I have strengths and weak points; I am wise sometimes, but I can be unbearably stupid too."

He says these things quietly but with visible passion.

"Grace was God's good gift to me," he insists. "I was young and very immature, not ready to be married. I didn't know how to be a good husband; I didn't know how to lead. I didn't know how to treat a woman…"

Jeremy is silent for a while, and we wait with him.

"I wasn't abusive or anything," he continues softly. "And I certainly wasn't sleeping around or cheating on Grace. It's just that…I was young. I had some definite ideas about a husband and his role. I had some strong opinions about a wife and her role.

"Grace had other ideas, but I really thought we were learning together. Then one day, she was just gone."

By prior arrangement, Jeremy's teen daughter, Marisa, joins us at this point in the interview. She strolls into the coffee shop with confidence, walks over to her dad, and hugs him. She jumps onto a bar stool beside her father, facing us across a small table.

"This is about divorce, right?" she asks us.

"Yes, but really it's about how to survive that and recover from it in healthy ways," we answer.

Marisa nods her head, seeming to consider the idea. "I don't think anybody ever recovers from it," she says without evident sadness in her voice. "I mean, how could you? You join your whole life with another person, and then they're gone. How exactly does someone 'recover' from that kind of a shock? I don't think it's possible."

Jeremy smiles. "She's bright, like her mother," he says, nodding at his daughter.

"I'm bright like both of you, Dad!" she insists unselfconsciously. "But seriously, I don't think anybody recovers from divorce, do they? I mean, people can go on with their lives, but do they ever really recover? Isn't there always this huge gaping hole in their hearts where their marriage used to be?"

"Marisa, you should think about becoming a counselor," Lisa suggests.

"I *am* thinking about it," she replies thoughtfully. "It's something I've kind of always had in the back of my mind. I'd like to help people who are going through the kinds of things I've been through, and my dad's been through. Even my mom, although she's the one who left us—her life hasn't been easy, either. I think I'd like being helpful, if I could."

We ask Marisa if she thinks her father ought to remarry.

"I used to really want him to," she says with a loud sigh. "He was so lonely all the time. I could see that even when I was little. He would just sit and stare off into space all the time. I mean, it wasn't healthy!"

Jeremy does not interject anything, so she continues. "After all, Dad has 'biblical grounds' for getting remarried. Mom left him; Mom has other men in her life. Actually, she's had lots of other men in her life. So if you ask me, Dad has God's permission to start over again with a new person. In my opinion, Dad has the right to get married again, and I think it would be a good choice for him, especially after I'm gone…

"But Dad—and I guess you've already heard him say this—doesn't see it like that. He says that 'permission' is not the same as 'God's first choice,' and somehow Dad believes that God's first choice is for him to wait on Mom to come back someday."

Does Marisa see that as a possibility?

"No way," she says quickly. "I haven't ever heard her even *talk* about getting back with Dad someday. I don't think she ever even considers that. She's moved on with her life. She's not thinking about the old days." Marisa shakes her head.

Jeremy interrupts his daughter for the first time. "Do you think I should get remarried now—so you'd have a mom in the house at this time in your life?" Jeremy asks her, watching for her reaction.

"I've already got a mom!" Marisa insists brightly. "But if you're asking me if you should date and stuff like that, I say yes. I think you need a woman in your life to cheer you up and make you happy. Daddy, when was the last time you were really truly happy?"

Jeremy ponders the question.

"He's a really good father," she continues. "He really is. He cares so much and he tries so hard and he gives me so much, even when he can't really afford to give it to me. Nobody could be a better father. I just wish he would date somebody, somebody who made him smile, somebody who played the guitar and sang crazy songs, somebody young and fun, maybe somebody who hadn't ever been married."

Jeremy rolls his eyes at this suggestion. "She used to say stuff like that all the time," he remarks. "She was always trying to play matchmaker, especially with the moms of her girlfriends. She has a lot of friends whose mothers are divorced and available—"

"And he wouldn't ever consider any of them," Marisa retorts, but kindly. "You know, the truth is, I really respect my dad for having his opinion. And it's not like other women don't find him attractive—I know they do. In fact, two of them are trying to get me to fix them up with him right now!"

She watches attentively for her father's response to this and pauses, expecting some sort of reaction.

Jeremy shakes his head but doesn't speak.

"So, anyway, I respect him for his opinion, I really do," Marisa adds quietly. "My dad is a person of strong convictions and really good moral values. He amazes me sometimes with how strong he is. I'm not that strong; I couldn't be alone all my life. I don't think I'd be willing to settle for that. I totally admire his opinion, and I also want him to change—isn't that crazy?" she muses. "I guess that's a screwed-up opinion, but it's exactly how I feel. You can write that if you want."

We do.

We save the last question for Jeremy, wanting to know if he believes he has done the right thing so far by staying single. And is it still the right thing?

His answer surprises us. "Right now, I really want what's best for Marisa, and I don't know what that is," he says softly. "I know I can't be all the things she needs right now. I've been trying to see this whole thing the way God sees it. I've been trying to make God happy and pleased with my life and my choices."

Though he has spoken softly and gently throughout this entire interview, he now lowers his voice even further. He hesitates before he speaks, seeming emotional. When he finally does speak again, his voice is tinged with sadness, perhaps regret.

He frames his words slowly. "But I have to tell you, honestly, even though I'm not changing my opinion—at least not yet…right now I find myself wanting what's best for Marisa in these next five or six years. If I honestly thought I could improve Marisa's life by getting remarried, I'd march up the aisle today. I don't know if I've done the right thing, but I know this—I love Marisa so much—if it would help her for me to get married, I'd do it in a heartbeat."

Jeremy's voice trails off into silence. There are tears in Marisa's eyes, and in other eyes also.

Divorce is like that.

Just when you think you've got an answer for something, another question springs up to surprise you.

Some Blessings of Flying Solo:
Life Lessons from Single Parents

Here are some of the advantages of staying single, as shown by the life experiences of Debbie and Jeremy in this chapter:

1. *Learning to rely on God; gaining a deeper spiritual life.* In a marriage relationship, you may rely on your spouse to take spiritual leadership in the home. When the partner is gone, there's no one to be the leader except you. Learning to lead wisely means learning how to pray, and growing in your ability to discern how God is guiding and directing you as you make choices for your family.

2. *Keeping "change" to a minimum.* There are already enough changes for your children to adjust to. Keeping your own home and lifestyle the same may help kids have a "constant" in their personal world. That consistency may reassure and help them.

3. *Becoming mature sooner.* Sometimes the presence of a relationship allows us to avoid the tough issues of life. We can let our partner manage money or decide how to discipline the kids. Being alone is a chance to "grow up" and function as an adult.

4. *Living out "God's first choice."* Some in the Christian community do not favor remarrying. Like Jeremy, they choose to believe that "patiently waiting" is God's first choice for them, regardless of what pathway their former partner chooses.

5. *Bonding more closely with your children.* Without a spouse or partner, your relationship with your children may become deeper and fuller. Even so, expect adolescents to pull away and strive for independence—it's natural.

Some Drawbacks of Flying Solo: Confessions from Single Parents

Here are some of the disadvantages of staying single, as related by those who are struggling to raise children on their own:

1. *Your children may lack another adult's perspective.* Children of divorce still have two parents; however, one of the parents may be living and behaving like a child or adolescent. As a single mother, you may wish for a godly man in the home as a role model, especially for your sons. As a single father, you may wish your daughter had a godly adult woman to lean on and learn from during the difficult transitions of the teen years.

2. *Living with loneliness and coping with depression alone.* Let's face it—children are no substitute for a life partner, nor are they intended to be. No matter how close you may become with your children, you will still feel alone. Different personalities respond differently to singleness—most divorced singles admit that life is lonely, especially around major holidays. Yet be sure of this: Marrying again to avoid loneliness may not be the pathway to personal happiness you expect.

3. *Welcome to your new lifestyle: poverty.* Two incomes are higher than one: This is simple math. In most cases, the income gain from combining two households exceeds the rise in expenses. Single parents are thrifty by necessity—there's never enough money to do everything, go everywhere, and keep up with the ongoing demands of life.

4. *Well-meaning friends may badger you with "help."* Your friends mean well; they want you to be happy. That's why they constantly annoy you with advice, suggestions, and possible relationships they hope you'll explore. Just be your own person: Don't allow your friends, despite their good intentions, to take you places you're not ready to go, emotionally or relationally.

Chapter Nine

Choosing to Remarry: Could It Be Right for You?

Moonlight and roses, but watch out for those thorns

We were not made to be alone.
As a woman, I was made to fit a man.
I feel most complete when I am part of two-in-one;
most whole when I am together in a marriage.
—Ginger, age 38, remarried

Tim and Janae got remarried less than three years after their divorces became final. Each of them brought children into the new family unit. Tim was busy caring for his three, Janae for her two. Their newly combined household contained five children under age 12.

In the preceding chapter, we looked at the choice of remaining single after divorce, particularly while raising younger children. We learned from the life experiences of two single parents—one father and one mother—who chose to raise their children alone, rather than marrying again. In this chapter, we'll look at two real-life stories of couples who chose to get remarried. We'll learn from their examples about the advantages as well as the difficulties of this. And we'll hear their own opinions about the wisdom of this particular decision.

Tim and Janae's Story

We begin with Tim and Janae because—right from the start—they experienced a high level of stress in their remarriage. Less than four months after saying "I do" in a small private ceremony, Tim lost his job. He'd worked for the same employer for more than 15 years; suddenly his job—his entire division—was outsourced. Here he was—newly married, heading a household of seven persons, and all at once he found himself unemployed.

"It was unbelievable," he says, remembering. "I mean, we'd heard some rumors about this before, but the rumors always proved to be false. Then without any warning, I showed up for work on Monday—and didn't have a job. I received exactly two weeks' severance pay, plus the company promised to help us prepare resumés and allow us to use their job-search database. Fifteen years of steady work for them, and my reward was…a job-search network?"

Tim was devastated, all the more so because he felt responsible for the care and feeding of a new wife and her two children, plus three of his own. "My first thought was, not only is *my* life going down the tubes, but now I'm taking Janae and her kids with me!" he exclaims, shaking his head. "I didn't want to go home, I didn't want to tell Janae—I just didn't want to deal with it."

Janae remembers it differently. "I was at work," she recalls. "I work at a large department store, and they paged me for a phone call, which is highly unusual. I took the call in the lower stockroom, and it was Tim telling me that he was suddenly unemployed. He sounded so calm on the phone, so matter-of-fact. I was impressed with his courage and his stability at that moment. I would have been crying!"

Tim...became a stay-at-home dad for the first time in his life. "He was good at it," Janae insists, smiling, "He's actually a good cook, better than I am."

Tim nods his head. "I *was* crying—but not so anyone could see it."

Inwardly, he was in full panic. He'd brought a high debt load into the new relationship and already felt guilty about inflicting it on Janae and her children. Janae—thrifty, careful, conservative—entered the new relationship debt-free, but with no savings or reserves.

"At that time, I was getting about 30 hours a week at the store," she explains. "That was the minimum level for keeping up my fully paid health-insurance plan. My work hours varied a lot, but I never let them go under 30 hours a week, because my kids and I needed that health insurance. I couldn't afford to pay for it on my own.

"When Tim lost his job, I sat down with my supervisor and explained what was happening. I asked if I could be scheduled for 40 hours a week anytime he could arrange that. I also asked that, if overtime was ever considered, could I please be scheduled for as much overtime as possible?"

Janae's supervisor responded by attempting to schedule her for a full 40 hours a week. In just a few weeks, she was reclassified as a full-time employee, although her hours and shifts varied widely. Tim, with his two weeks' severance pay, became a stay-at-home dad for the first time in his life.

"He was good at it," Janae insists, smiling. "He's actually a good cook, better than I am. And at that time Crystal was not in pre-K yet. I would have a friend watch her for a little pay while I was at work. So when Tim lost his job, we quit paying my friend. He stayed at home and watched Crystal."

Not that Janae abandoned her homemaking altogether. "I still did the morning routines—breakfast for everyone, lunches for the kids for school—but after that, Tim ran the household while I went off for a full day at work. My hours changed every day, but I never started before 10 AM.

"That gave us 'family time' in the mornings—a crazy, hectic time to be together, with everyone rushing to get ready for school—but at least we were in the same house at the same time during those mornings."

On the job front, however, things went from bad to worse.

"I think the worst of it was about six months later," Tim recalls. "I had been out of work that whole period, looking for jobs, sending out resumés—and I had gotten maybe three interviews during all that time, but no callbacks. I had gained about 15 pounds being unemployed. I was eating a lot because I was so depressed. I was depressed a lot because I couldn't find any company that was hiring—or even the possibility of a good-paying job.

"I don't know why Janae stayed with me then, or how she put up with me for all that time. I was getting calls from creditors because I wasn't making the payments that were due. My truck almost got repoed."

Janae gets quiet. "I was losing him," she says after a long pause. "Every day he kind of sank lower and lower into the pit. He quit laughing and joking. He was tense and nervous—the least little thing would upset him.

"My kids, who didn't know him very well yet, stayed away from him during that time. They didn't know what to think. I wasn't always sure either. I sometimes wondered if I'd done the right thing," she admits. "Some of my friends had told me I was getting married 'too soon'— whatever that is. But by then I'd been divorced for three years. Tim and I had dated for about eight months and we knew each other really well. I thought I was ready...

"What I wasn't ready for," she continues after a moment's reflection, "was a husband who was depressed all the time, out of work, losing his self-confidence daily. He was getting less and less sure of himself. He was a lot less cheerful and positive. Really—in a lot of ways—he wasn't the same guy I had agreed to marry. He was very different from when we were dating."

Tim appears to agree entirely.

"If I had been married to me, *I* would have left me!" he insists. "I was pretty much a basket case. I stayed brave around my kids and kept telling them not to worry. I don't know if *they* believed me or not—but *I* didn't believe me. I was worried sick, gaining weight. No matter what I tried, I couldn't find any real work, just little odd jobs that paid a few bucks here and there. Every day that went by I sank a little lower into depression and guilt."

Had their pre-remarriage counseling prepared them for this possibility?

"We didn't have any pre-remarriage counseling." Janae grimaces. "The minister really wanted us to, but we kept putting him off. We were both working, we were both single parents, so we didn't really think we had any extra time for any counseling sessions. We kept turning down every time slot that the minister would offer us, and we always had a good reason. Finally, the pastor just quit calling us. I think he realized we were a lost cause.

"I wasn't too worried about that, because I'd had premarriage counseling before my first marriage, and look how that turned out! So neither of us really tried very hard to be available for counseling before our remarriage."

Tim agrees. "Maybe it would have helped us," he sighs. "But back then, we were both so busy, it just wasn't a priority for us. Besides, how would a minister—or anyone outside our relationship—know what was best for the two of us?"

As they struggled to keep the marriage together, how did things eventually work out for Tim with regard to his employment? What opportunity did he eventually find? How did their prayers for employment finally get answered?

Long before any real doors opened, Janae says, she had an epiphany. "I was driving home from the store," she remembers. "And I was praying Tim would find work, just like I always did. And all of a sudden, I just got this very calm sense about it, this deep peaceful feeling. I didn't hear any voices, no great ideas formed in my brain, I didn't hear God 'talking to me' or anything like that. I was just driving and praying—and suddenly I was flooded with a huge sense of peacefulness and calmness about Tim's job search, our financial needs, the whole thing.

"By the time I got home, I really wasn't worried about it anymore, at least not as worried as I had been. I couldn't explain it, and I wasn't ready to talk to anyone about it, including Tim. But I knew everything had changed—at least everything inside of me, my emotions— had changed. I had a true and genuine sense of peace. I knew God was at work to do something good for us.

"Later I realized Tim would have lost his job either way, whether he married me or not. I was able to separate Tim's unemployment issues from the fact the two of us had decided to get married. That thought, also, came to me while I was praying and driving. It just sort of formed in my brain. You wouldn't believe how much that idea helped me. It was like, Tim would be going through this anyway—it still would have happened—but now we can share it together, work through it together, and maybe be stronger as a family because of going through all this."

Tim firmly believes the same thing. "She didn't tell me those feelings right away. But a few days later she sat down and told me she'd been praying, and God had given her a great sense of peace. And somehow just the way she told me that—I got a lot of peace just by hearing her say that. I felt like the weight of the world was starting to lift off my shoulders for the first time."

Eventually, after eight months of fruitlessly searching for available jobs, Tim was hired by a man from his church. Instead of continuing to do drafting and engineering for a living, Tim was now in sales. It was a major change.

"By then, I was ready for anything," Tim declares. "I'd never thought of myself as a salesman before, but I was ready to do anything, anywhere, if there was a chance of making decent money at it. Jerry showed me, on paper, what my commissions might be, using a very conservative set of sales numbers. He was very convincing. He told me I could be good at sales just by being honest and direct with people. I didn't have to have some special kind of outgoing personality or anything. I didn't have to be the life of the party."

Did the job change work out well? Did things improve for the couple? If so, how long did it take, and how did it happen?

"It's been up and down," Tim acknowledges. "But overall, I'm probably back to making about what I made before I lost my job. So basically I've replaced my income from before, and I'm actually starting to enjoy what I do for a living. Overall, that's made me a lot more positive than I was. I've started to believe in myself again. I've just finished setting some goals with Jerry that will really help this family if I can achieve them. And Jerry's strength is helping me make concrete, workable plans that can turn those goals into reality."

Janae has the same opinion. "Tim has his confidence back," she relates. "He pulls into the driveway, and there's a spring in his step when he comes through the door. He whistles now—we didn't hear him whistle for about a year there, it seems like. These days we all see him happier, more relaxed, more himself."

Given the difficulties they faced—the financial stresses, the long period of unemployment for Tim—would they do things differently, knowing what they know now? Would they wait longer to get married knowing that a lot of hardship and adversity was waiting for them, so early in the new relationship?

"I don't know," Janae says, pondering the question. "I mean, if you wait until you're certain about everything, you'll never make a decision. I think we both knew we loved each other. Both of us had negative experiences from our first marriages, so both of us were ready to make it work for us, whatever it took."

Tim's view differs here. "I wouldn't have put her through all that," he insists. "If I'd known I was going to lose my job, I would never have proposed marriage to a beautiful woman with two young children to raise. I mean, how irresponsible is that?"

He reflects for a moment. "But I'll tell you something. Since it happened anyway, I'm really glad I didn't have to go through it alone. I mean, I had my kids and everything, but you don't exactly sit down among your kids and process your depression, you know? I was busy trying to be brave for my kids; I needed somebody to be brave for me! It was so helpful to have Janae there…"

Janae dabs at a tear. She tries to speak, then pauses to compose herself before framing her thoughts into words. "There were days and weeks there, even months, when I didn't think we were going to make it. I would think to myself—*Here I go again, I'm heading for another divorce, another broken relationship.*

"In the end, it brought us closer together though," she says. "Not that I wish it happened—I wouldn't wish that on anybody. But the truth is, by going through all of that, it brought us closer together. It's made our relationship stronger and closer and deeper just by going through it."

Tim agrees. "The closeness we have now, the sense of 'forever' we feel about our marriage and our relationship—I'm not sure we'd have that if it wasn't for all we've been through together."

Hand in hand, the couple smile at each other. To anyone looking on, they seem for all the world like a long-term, first-marriage couple sharing the joys of a lengthy and fulfilling partnership.

Roger and Megan's Story

Sudden adversity is also a factor in our second life story. Once again, a newly remarried couple confronted issues that challenged their ability to survive as a lasting union. While not typical of most remarriages, this story is included precisely because it highlights the kinds of issues most couples don't fully consider as they think about remarrying and forming a new family.

Marrying after a brief courtship, Roger and Megan had fewer children to raise than Tim and Janae. Roger, divorced nearly ten years, had grown children who lived on their own. Megan, divorced only a year or so when she started dating Roger, was raising three young children under the age of seven. Megan's ex-husband had moved out of state, back home with his parents about eight hours away. For all practical purposes, he was not involved in the lives of his children.

Roger and Megan experienced a sudden rush of "falling in love."

Certain they were meant to be together, they planned a wedding and accomplished a remarriage less than four months after they first met. All at once, they were setting up a new household and forming a new family unit.

Roger remembers the transition time as being exceptionally difficult. "Megan's kids seemed to accept me while we were dating. But somehow when I moved in with them, everything changed. I don't know how or why, but the kids were *less* responsive to me instead of being more so. I thought my relationship with the kids would improve once I lived there and was part of the family. In fact, everything just got harder."

Then things got substantially more difficult. Driving home from the movies one Saturday afternoon, Megan sensed a tenderness in her left breast. Exploring it further after getting home, she felt a large lump— every woman's worst nightmare.

"It was malignant," she says. "It was malignant and fast-growing, and it came out of nowhere. I mean, there's no history of cancer in my family at all, not in the women, not in the men, not anywhere. I've never been a smoker, I'm a salad eater—who knew I could get cancer, and so suddenly?"

Roger has a theory about that. "There's this huge link between emotional stress and physical health," he notes. "I keep reading more and more about that all the time. Megan had been through this really messy divorce, she was so stressed out—I think her stress may have weakened her immune system, maybe even caused the cancer."

Regardless of the causes, Megan's prognosis seemed desperate.

"They were worried about the cancer spreading," she remembers. "Because it was so fast-growing and attacked me so suddenly, they were worried it was going to migrate to other parts of my body and attack me there."

Megan's doctor scheduled surgery immediately but also wanted a full regimen of other treatments. For Megan, it seemed she was glowing with health one day and sagging under horrible treatments and side effects the next.

"I was miserable," she sighs. "And although I tried not to act like it, I was also terribly afraid. I know God is supposed to be 'with us' at times like that, but I'll tell you the truth—I was just plain scared. I thought I was dying, and I wondered what was going to happen to my kids. My kids didn't seem to even *like* Roger in those early days of our marriage. What was going to happen to Roger? What was going to happen to my three kids? I lay awake at night, sick to my stomach from all the treatments and worried about how my new family was going to get along after I died."

The thought that her ex-husband might somehow end up raising her children was what kept Megan fighting the cancer all the way.

"Absolutely." She grins. "I could handle the dying part, but letting Bobby raise my kids? No way!"

For 18 months, the status of Megan's health was unclear. Doctors were convinced that, although the surgery seemed to remove all visible evidence of the tumors, the fast-growing nature of the cancer made it likely to recur.

"Roger turned into 'Mr. Mom' through all that," Megan reports. "He kept working because we couldn't afford for him not to. But he'd get up before work and do breakfast and get the kids ready. He'd come home from work and start cleaning the house. He'd make dinner for everybody most nights."

These are not exactly Roger's areas of giftedness. "No," he admits wryly, "I'm not a cook, and cleaning the house has never been very high on my list of priorities. But it needed to be done, and in an odd way, it was kind of like therapy for me. Staying busy helped me not have time to worry so much. Otherwise I would spend most of my time worrying."

Megan worried too. "I know I should have grown spiritually through all of that," she says today. "But to be honest with you, I was pretty mad at God. I couldn't understand why God would want to kill me, frankly, and I couldn't understand how God could put my kids through all that—or maybe let them end up back with Bobby. How could that possibly be God's plan for my life, and for theirs?"

"I was mad at God too," Roger confesses. "I had already lost one wife to divorce, now it seemed like I was losing another one to cancer. What did I ever do to God that He would take two wives away from me?"

Megan returns to her narrative. "So anyway—I'm embarrassed to admit this—but I didn't grow much spiritually or become mature in Christ. I know I should have! But what actually did happen is that Roger and I got a lot closer through all of that suffering."

Roger nods. "On her worst days," he says softly, "when she really didn't have any energy or any joy, when she would just withdraw—even on those days I was so grateful to still have a wife…"

Megan reaches for his hand.

Knowing what they know now, would they still get remarried? Would they make the same decisions again, realizing how the future would turn out? Would they take the same steps, even understanding the risks in advance?

"No," Megan declares. "I mean, what kind of marriage proposal would that be: 'I've got cancer, will you marry me?' I wouldn't have let Roger get so close to me, let alone marry me, if I'd known what I was facing. I would not have gotten remarried, not to Roger or anyone else. But I don't know what I would have done with my kids while I went through surgery and treatment. That's what would have really worried me. Who would have taken care of my kids through all that?"

Roger sees a virtue in Megan's suffering, albeit a bittersweet one. "She needed me," he says about the season of cancer and treatments. "Before that, I couldn't see how she needed me. She was young and strong and just seemed so successful and well-adjusted. I thought maybe she only needed me to help with the kids, but obviously the kids weren't ready to accept my help when we first got married. They shunned me and didn't seem to like me.

"Then, when the cancer hit her, the kids really didn't have any kind of support network except me. When they fell down and got hurt, I was the one taking care of them. When they got scared in the middle of the night, I was the one calming them down. I cooked, I cleaned, I watched over them. I turned into their father and mother combined, and I was only a brand-new stepdad," he sighs. "But cancer is like that. It really knocked Megan down for a while. It almost knocked her out completely."

> "It really is true that having cancer, and me being so weak and incapable, helped Roger and me build our relationship deeper...We grew together a lot more quickly than we would have."

"So you would have married me, knowing I had cancer?" Megan asks.

Roger is pensive. "Well, I'd like to think so, but I'm not so sure. It would have been a lot to think about before getting married. I think I would have been so afraid of losing a second wife that maybe I would have held back and not let myself get involved."

Megan nods in agreement. "Exactly. Both of us would have held back from each other, rather than letting things get as far as marriage. I think a lot of divorced people go around 'holding back' anyway because they're so afraid of being hurt, so afraid everything will collapse around them."

Yet Roger and Megan did get married, not knowing what they were about to experience. Would they do anything differently, looking back?

"I would say no to a lot of the treatments," Megan shares. "I know the doctors were worried, but I went through a lot more from the treatments than I ever did from the cancer itself. Having those treatments was horrible."

She has been symptom-free for more than five years. Is she worried about the cancer returning someday?

"It's something I think about, obviously," she admits. "I mean, once you've been through that, I don't think you ever really relax. But it really is true that having cancer, and me being so weak and incapable, helped Roger and me build our relationship deeper. We formed new patterns of trusting and helping each other. We grew together a lot more quickly than we would have. Who knows? Maybe without the cancer, the remarriage wouldn't have worked…"

Roger gets the last word. "Having watched her go through all that, I'd rather be married and fighting—like we might have been otherwise—than have the great relationship we have today, if cancer was what it took to get us that great relationship. I'm grateful for how close we are. And both of us are learning how to trust God—we're growing up a little bit, maybe, in our walk with God. But who would ever choose cancer as a way of deepening a marriage relationship?"

The Potential Reward

These two real-life stories are starker than most: the loss of a job, the loss of physical health. Not every remarriage will be tested in such severe ways. Most remarried couples encounter stresses that are more typical, such as financial strain, difficult relationships with ex-partners, and discipline problems with the children.

Yet the stories in this chapter remind us that the future is uncertain. We may lose our jobs, our financial security, and our health. Our new partner may be suddenly stricken—we may find ourselves serving as caregivers just when we expected to be enjoying the glow of a "honeymoon phase." We do not—and we cannot—know the future.

Life is like that.

For many divorced people, one of the primary benefits of getting remarried is exactly what these two experiences highlight: If there is suffering on the road ahead, it seems good to have a partner at our side for support and help.

"I know I should have relied on God for everything while I was sick," Megan said at one point near the close of our interview. "But I think the way God chose to take care of me was by putting Roger into my life."

As we walk toward an uncertain future, some of us find value in making the journey hand in hand, with a partner at our side. For those of us who do so, despite the stresses involved, the potential reward is a meaningful and lasting friendship—a healthy and fulfilling marriage that goes the distance, lasting for a lifetime filling the future with purpose and joy.

Advantages of Choosing Remarriage:
Life Lessons from Remarried Couples

Here are some of the advantages of remarrying, as illustrated by the life experiences of the couples in this chapter:

1. *Learning to give of yourself in new ways.* You may not have prepared yourself to be a housekeeper, cook, or nurse's aide, but life may have other plans. Because of the surprises life may bring, you may find yourself in roles that are surprising and challenging. Yet these things that stretch you may bring the two of you together deeply and meaningfully.

2. *Facing difficulty together, not alone.* Losing a job, finding a cancerous lump—these are difficult and challenging stresses for anyone. Yet having a partner at your side may be just the steadying influence you need. It's tough to be alone when you're healthy and employed. When you lose the things that form your support, having a partner is priceless.

3. *Modeling success for a family that's known failure.* The end of a previous marriage may leave children unsure of the value of committed relationships, or uncertain that promises made can be promises kept. Showing your children a healthy union, one that fulfills and keeps the promises of marriage, can help them find a new and positive perspective on family life.

4. *Two parents may be better than one.* In the wrestling match of raising confident and healthy kids, sometimes it's easier to enter as a tag-team. Two of you can take turns dealing with the stresses and challenges of parenting. When only one parent is on duty, it may seem like that one parent is always tired, always near or at the point of exhaustion. With two parents in the home, you can divide the duties—and conquer.

Disadvantages of Choosing Remarriage: What to Consider Before the Ceremony

Here are some of the disadvantages of remarrying, as suggested by the life experiences of the two couples in this chapter:

1. *Increased financial pressure and stress.* Adding a partner and perhaps a partner's children to the list of those you support each month may cause you additional stress and worry, especially if your job does not seem secure or stable. With corporations downsizing, outsourcing, and regrouping, even long-term jobs may be lost suddenly.

2. *Your partner's children may not be ready to accept you.* Even if you're wise enough to resist "replacing" the father or mother of your partner's children, the children may reject you and see you as a threat or a challenge to their other parent. You may have a wonderful relationship with your new partner, yet you may endure constant stress and opposition from that partner's kids.

3. *One or both of you may become incapacitated.* An auto accident, the sudden onset of cancer—life's surprises can catch us with calamity and loss. You marry with at least a tacit expectation of "happily ever after," and yet there is a very real possibility of suffering and loss, even early in the new marriage relationship. Are you prepared to lose a spouse?

4. *People change as a result of difficult circumstances.* The whistling optimist you marry today may be the sullen pessimist that shares your breakfast tomorrow. Sometimes the circumstances of life weigh us down. Over time, a personality can change; a basic temperament adjusts as a response to sad realities. We may literally become different persons; our spouse may change as well.

PART FOUR

*After Divorce—
Where to Find Help and Hope*

CHAPTER TEN

Household Management: Learning What You Don't Know

MOVING FROM CLUELESSNESS TO COMPETENCE

I change my own oil now, and I know what I'm doing!
I always felt vaguely guilty (while I was married) about not
knowing how to repair the car, fix things around the house,
or find my way around a Home Depot store.
Well, guess what? I do now!
—Meredith, age 28, divorced mother of two

Derek and Cindy had been married for three years before he left her. Cindy came home from work one day and discovered that Derek's clothes were missing from their closet. His computer and stereo equipment were missing from the den. One more thing was also missing: Derek himself.

She hadn't seen it coming.

"We weren't really happy," she says today, "and I knew that. But we were doing as well as any other married couple we knew. We didn't fight much, we had just bought a house—I thought things were pretty good for us."

Derek, apparently, had other ideas. Cindy later learned he had been "dating" someone else for nearly all of their three-year marriage. The discovery of his secret nearly crushed his young wife.

"I had a good job," she says, looking back. "And I had a great support network of friends at the office. Otherwise, I don't know how I would have made it through those days…"

Her husband filed for the divorce. After learning about the other woman, and especially about the fact he had been with the other person throughout most of their marriage, Cindy was not inclined to stand by her man.

"He made his choice," she says with resignation in her voice. "Maybe if it had been a one-night stand or something, I would have fought harder to save our marriage. But this had been going on almost the whole time we'd been together!"

The divorce filing was reasonably generous. Cindy received the house—and of course the mortgage along with it. Derek kept his own truck (he had never added Cindy's name to the title) and his own belongings. Otherwise, the home and its furnishings were Cindy's—as was their second car, an older Volvo.

"We had bought a fixer in a solid neighborhood," Cindy recalls, describing the house she purchased with her husband. "We closed on it about eight months before Derek left me. We hadn't gotten around to doing much of the fixing yet."

Cindy knew nothing at all about home repair, and even less about how to keep an older Volvo running during a cold Northwest winter. "I felt helpless at first," she remembers. "I was in shock about the affair, confused about the divorce, and just generally clueless about how to take care of anything—the house, the car, or any of our appliances."

More Than Receiving Help—Learning Self-Reliance

Cindy received help from an unlikely source: Derek's father.

"Derek's parents were so great with me," she sighs. "It's like they both felt so bad about what Derek had done, about what he was doing. Both of them, his mom and his dad, were totally helpful to me when I needed it the most."

Derek's father, an experienced trim carpenter and home repairman, volunteered to help Cindy remodel the house and prepare it for sale. He offered to completely check the Volvo for any needed repairs and then fix it himself if he was able to do so. Otherwise, he would be glad to help with any costs.

"I told him, 'Don't just fix it for me, show me how to do it myself!'" Cindy says with a laugh. "I didn't want to go from being so dependent on Derek to being equally dependent on his father. What good would that do?"

Jimmy, Derek's father, agreed, patiently teaching her how to do basic home repair and remodeling projects. After two months of working with her, he bought her a fairly complete set of her own tools.

"I cried," Cindy says with emotion in her voice. "He was already being so nice about everything. Then when he bought me those tools and gave them to me as a gift, I just sat down on the floor and cried. It was so sweet!"

How did Jimmy respond?

Cindy laughs. "I'm not sure he realized I was happy," she notes. "I think maybe he thought he had offended me or something. I was just weeping away, crying up a storm. Jimmy looked worried at first."

So has Cindy learned how to use all those new tools?

"Jimmy taught me so much," she says with much gratitude in her voice. "He was very patient, very slow—I wasn't exactly a good student. A lot of times I had no idea what he had just told me. And often my mind was wandering since I was still so depressed about the whole divorce thing. So I was a pretty slow learner, but he stuck with me. He didn't give up; he didn't seem frustrated."

Jimmy patiently trained Cindy in the basics of home remodeling and auto repair. Along the way, both he and Derek's mother, Carol, bonded with Cindy, letting her know they were "there for her" in any way she needed.

"I remember coming home one day after a hard day at the office, and I went outside to check the mailbox. When I did, there was note waiting for me from Jimmy and Carol. Inside the envelope was a funny card, plus a gift certificate to Safeway. They were giving me $100 worth of groceries in the form of a gift certificate.

"I don't know if they had looked around my house or not." Cindy smiles. "But their timing was perfect. I was out of everything! I hadn't really adjusted to just cooking for myself. It's so weird—after coming home every day and making dinner for two people, it was hard to come home and make a meal for only one."

> Cindy's confidence is evident…She's been given
> the tools to care for her home and her car,
> all by herself if neccessary.

What did she buy with the grocery-store gift certificate?

"Mostly microwaveable stuff," she confesses with a laugh. "For that whole first year or so, I basically lived on microwave burritos, microwave omelettes, microwave soup. I still had nice wedding gifts, including a lot of wonderful cookware—but I just couldn't get excited about spending an hour in the kitchen to cook for just me."

Although Cindy had been deserted by her husband, she was being supported by her ex-husband's parents. She expresses a gratitude for their help—it's a debt, she says, she'll never be able to repay.

"We've got a real friendship now," she says. "I love both of them, and I know both of them love me. We never talk about Derek—what is there to say?—but I know both of Derek's parents love me, and they always will."

Brimming with confidence, Cindy says she's now unafraid of something breaking at her house, or of the car suddenly needing repairs or maintenance. "If I can't handle it, Jimmy probably can. And if he can't handle it, at least I'll know I'm not being taken advantage of. Jimmy is a good judge of how much car repair ought to cost and whether or not someone is being honest."

Cindy plans to keep the house and to keep on fixing it. "Are you kidding?" she asks when we raise the question. "I'm building equity in this place every single day. Or more accurately, the work Jimmy is helping me to do, and training me to do, is building equity in this house every day. Since the divorce, this house has gone up in value by at least 20 percent."

We ask Cindy about her comfort level with car repair.

"Well, I'm thinking about buying an older Honda or Toyota." She smiles as she responds. "No offense to my present fine car, but if I'm going to be the one responsible for repairs, I'd like to do fewer of them. Jimmy says Honda and Toyota are the most reliable car brands, and he probably knows what he's talking about. So I may drive this Volvo for a while yet, then look around for an older Accord or Camry."

Cindy's confidence is evident as she talks freely about car makes, reliability issues, and her possible future purchases. No longer depending on a husband for the routine maintenance issues of life, she's been given the tools to care for her home and her car, all by herself if necessary.

Financial Management for the Fiscally Unprepared

When Paul left Melinda, he took the checkbook with him.

It wouldn't have mattered if he'd left it behind. Melinda had rarely seen it; she had never been involved in balancing it. Paul paid the bills, managed the money, and ran the financial aspects of their marriage as a one-man show. When he left, the money manager was missing from the home.

Melinda, facing an unexpected divorce, was clueless about her finances. "I didn't know anything," she says today. "That's not exaggeration, that's just a fact. I didn't know a credit card from a debit card. I didn't know how to set up a direct deposit for my paycheck. I had no idea how much our utility costs were or how those bills got paid. Paul used a program called Quicken to manage all our household expenses, but it was loaded on his laptop computer. When he left me, he took that computer with him. I didn't have any files, records, printouts, or anything else that explained to me how much money I had or where it might be."

Melinda sought help immediately, calling a friend who worked as an accountant for a small company. "She told me about a class at a nearby church. The class was designed for widows who were suddenly alone, to help them learn how to run their finances and pay their bills. I felt a little awkward calling the church office, asking if I could be included in their finance class. I wasn't a widow—at least not in the usual sense. But I needed help, and I needed it right away!"

By divine providence, the next class was beginning soon. Melinda purchased two books, using money she borrowed from her mother. "At first, I just lived on whatever my parents gave me," she recalls. "And my dad helped me set up a bank account in my name and theirs so I could have access to money while I figured everything out."

The finance class was a video-based course featuring a well-known Christian financial manager. For Melinda, it was absolutely life-changing.

"Oh," she says, talking about the course, "it was the best thing that happened to me in those horrible days right after the divorce. That class was a lifesaver—and before I got into it, I was definitely drowning!"

In simple, nonthreatening lessons, she learned how to establish, run, and adjust a household budget. The forms she needed were included in the books and course materials she purchased from the church bookstore.

"It probably would have been smarter to set things up online, like my husband had been doing," she admits. "But at that time I didn't even have a computer! I knew a few programs, like Microsoft Word, but I had never done anything financial on a computer. I had hardly even used an ATM machine."

Melinda was a good student, capably learning the lessons as they were presented. A live instructor led discussions after each video lesson, then the course participants did exercises in their workbooks while in the room. She found herself helping the widows, many of whom were much more than twice her age, as they confronted debits, subtotals, expense ledgers, and other kinds of worksheets in their course materials.

"Here I was, helping other people, and I hardly even knew what I was doing," she remarks with a smile. "But at least I could use an adding machine. And I could read and understand the forms. Some of those ladies were visually impaired, so I had to read the instructions to them out loud."

By the time the course ended, Melinda was feeling much more confident. "I bought a few other books by the same author—using my parents' money, which was normal right then. I learned so much about how to wisely manage money—things I had never known before."

Today, although she admits that money is "tight," she is running her own household using the same program—Quicken—that her ex-husband was so fond of. She's become computer-literate in addition to learning how to manage a household budget.

"It was that same church," she laughs. "They were having a seminar on how to use computers, and for that one you didn't have to be a widow. Of course I signed up, and I learned a lot during the class. By the time it was over, my dad took me shopping for an inexpensive computer system. He paid less than $500 but bought me a computer, monitor, and printer for that. Is my dad a smart shopper, or what?"

The Struggle with Housework and Cooking: True Confessions of "The Cereal Dad"

Roman shares custody of his two school-age children. It's not the life he imagined during the summer of 1995, when he proposed to his high-school sweetheart.

"I thought we would be together forever." He sighs. "And if it was up to me, we would be. Divorce teaches you to expect surprises, though—both good and bad!"

Roman was surprised by how much he didn't know about household tasks.

"Look, I grew up in a traditional home—is that wrong?" he wonders. "Dad went to work in the morning and came home every day at the same time. Mom was the one who cooked, cleaned, and ran the family. That's what I learned growing up."

What Roman didn't learn included quite a few things: how to wash clothes, how to do ironing, how to cook, how to clean up the kitchen after cooking, and more. He's having to teach himself those skills now, as a direct consequence of finding himself divorced.

What is he learning by living on his own and sharing custody of two young children?

"For one thing, I was a slob while I was married," he now realizes. "I should have helped take care of the chores. I should have at least cleaned up after myself. I fell into the same patterns I learned growing up—dads go to work, moms cook the meals."

How does Roman handle basic duties like meal preparation now that he's alone?

He laughs out loud. "I'm a cereal father." He grins. "My kids eat a lot of cereal at my house."

Beyond cereal, the divorced dad's talents include frozen waffles and spaghetti—and taking the kids out for fast food. "We do that way too much," he confesses, "but you have to admit, those people aren't just selling food, they're selling entertainment! My two can kill several hours in those play areas. The big challenge is getting them to eat while they're in the restaurant…"

What's been the hardest thing for him to learn, household-wise?

"Ironing," Roman grimaces. "I'm still not doing it right. I mean, why is the ironing board shaped that way? Did somebody make it that shape on purpose? I can't figure out how the shape of the ironing board is supposed to help me."

Roman wonders if his experience is typical of divorced fathers.

"Is this what all of us are going through?" he asks aloud. "And if it is, where are the classes to help divorced dads learn all the stuff we need to know?"

That's a question well worth asking.

Lifelines for Parents As Well

Doreen, divorced and the mother of two teens, needed help coping with the constant challenges to her authority she faced at home. Her sons not only didn't pay attention to her—they often insulted her, laughing at her to her face. Flustered by this show of rebellion, she didn't know how to respond.

When a course called "Support for Parents of Adolescents" was offered at a nearby church, she was literally the first person who called to enroll.

"If they were offering any real support, I knew I needed it," she says.

Fourteen other parents were in the first session. Doreen was one of only two divorced persons; the other class members were married. "Parenting teens is parenting teens," she comments today. "And I didn't have a clue. I felt helpless, ignored, disrespected in my own home. I knew it was wrong, but I didn't have the slightest idea how to fix it!"

What were her thoughts as the class began?

"The same thing I always thought," she confesses. "Mostly that I wished I could get married so a man could make my children obey me!"

Doreen didn't get married, but she did gain the respect and obedience of her teen boys. She did so by following the principles and precepts that were explained in the course for parents of adolescents. "That first night," she recalls, "the one thing I remember was when the instructor had us all say together out loud—we can't be doing *everything* wrong!—And we all laughed so hard at that. We needed to laugh that night. Most of us were so burnt out, so frustrated by the lack of cooperation from our kids. The instructor managed to convince us, in just one session, that we were probably doing a few things right. We weren't the total failures we all felt like we were."

Doreen's confidence increased, but so too did her competence. She began to define her boundaries and insist on being treated with politeness and respect. When respect didn't happen, consequences did. "That first time I took away the car keys, they couldn't believe it. Only one of them could drive, but both of them usually grabbed the keys and went out driving around together, regardless of whether or not they had permission from me to be out running around."

Their mother was serious. "They stared at me like I must be kidding. They started talking about finding the spare set of keys and going out anyway. So I told them the truth—if they got in that car somehow and drove away, I was calling the police and reporting the car as stolen. They could make their explanations to the police, as far as I was concerned."

Doreen wasn't bluffing, and somehow her sons figured that out. It was the beginning of a substantial change in their relationship with their mother, a relationship that soon began to show evidence of a growing mutual respect.

"They didn't become perfect little darlings," Doreen states. "They were the same troublemakers they always had been since their dad left us. But at least they were respecting my rules and treating me better. I didn't feel like such a total failure as a mom. I knew I was making progress, even if it was slow."

She has been back to the class, cycling through the same material three times in a row. She says it helps her learn and remember the material. "It's not like I don't still need help," she declares. "Every time I go to that class, I end up learning from it—even if I've already heard the same lesson once or twice before. I feel better about myself as a mother. I feel better about my sons and their ability to treat adults with respect.

"Let's face it—I just feel better!"

Whether the topic is home remodeling, car repair, financial management, or the care and feeding of angry adolescents, resources for divorced parents are as near as a family member, a close friend, an employer, or a neighborhood church. Much help is available freely or inexpensively.

Many times, all that's missing is an awareness of what's available. A great place to start is the bookstore, library, or office of a large church. If you have access to a church of several-thousand-plus members, it's a great place to browse for resources, classes, books, and help of every kind.

If your community is smaller, find a library and go online, looking for classes and options that may be offered by a community college or a nearby vocational school. In many communities, even comparatively smaller churches offer car-repair days, computer training courses, and other help for divorced persons and single parents.

If you're struggling with an area of household or family management, feeling clueless and largely inept—join the club. Many divorced people feel the same way. That's exactly why so many resources are being offered these days.

Where to Shop for the Tools You Need

Here are some tips for finding help with some of the major challenges of household management. If you have access to the Internet, live near a public library, or watch cable television, the solutions you need may be closer than you realize!

Financial Planning and Budgeting

Whether your challenge is getting out of debt, learning to live on a budget, or setting up a way to pay bills, your local library or bookstore is packed with titles that can help. Some of these are in the For Dummies series—yellow covers with black titles.

On the Web, two sources of financial advice from a Christian viewpoint are Crown Ministries and Ronald Blue & Company.* Their sites can provide a wealth of useful information and link you to other sources of assistance. See the resources section at the back of this book for more information.

Even if you're not computer-savvy, current software programs such as Quicken are widely popular because they're easy to use. Balancing your checkbook, tracking your credit-card payments, making sure routine bills get paid on time—these and other chores can be simpler with a little on-screen help and encouragement. Your bank or credit union may offer some of these same services and programs as part of their checking or savings account packages.

Auto Maintenance and Repair

Even if you're not driving a mostly new car, consider talking to your local auto dealership. Some dealers offer basic car-maintenance classes, often free of charge and scheduled for Saturdays or weekday evenings.

Many of these courses are designed to teach you about your recent purchase (such as that new Honda Civic in your driveway), but others are more general in nature. You'll learn how to check your oil, change a flat tire, and perform routine maintenance.

Community colleges are also great sources of information and

---

* Respectively, www.crown.org and www.ronblue.com.

training about auto maintenance and repair. While there may be a small fee to take a class, most community colleges are affordable places to acquire the skills you need. Classes are generally in the afternoon or evening, designed to accommodate the schedules of working adults.

Brushing Up Your Computer Skills

Need to refresh your computer skills or learn how to use a program like Microsoft's Publisher or PowerPoint? As a first step, check out your local computer store or office supply company.

Many locations of FedEx Kinko's can guide you to classes, often held on-site, that help you learn specific programs or general computing skills. Big office-supply stores such as Staples and Office Depot may also refer you to useful classes and training, often free of charge.

Computer stores such as Best Buy, CompUSA, and Circuit City can be great places to ask about classes and training. Many stores offer in-aisle or on-site training, sometimes led by representatives of the major computer manufacturers. Major computer brands are often good sources for free or low-priced classes in how to use their equipment.

You may also find computer-skill classes available at your local church or at one of the larger congregations in your community. Adult-education programs supported by your park service, county, or community college also feature computer training as a prominent part of their free or low-fee educational options.

Home Maintenance and Repair

Owing partly to the popularity of cable-TV series such as *This Old House,* home-repair and home-remodeling training is widely available on-screen and online. If you have basic cable service, sit down with your channel guide and look at the community access channels and specialty channels that are part of your package.

You may be surprised to find TV programs that cover exactly what you're trying to learn or accomplish! You can record the show if you're at work, then watch it at your own pace and learn on your own schedule. The better programs are slow, step-by-step, visual guides to basic processes such as repairing a leaky faucet, finding and fixing a problem with your toilet, or similar challenges.

Big-box warehouse stores such as Lowe's and Home Depot are also great places to find classes. Many of them are free, designed to show you how to use all those tools and supplies the store is selling! But whether you shop there or not, consider showing up for a class and learning a new skill.

Who knows? Maybe instead of becoming a handyman, you'll meet one!

Chapter Eleven

Pilgrims' Progress:
A Divorce Roundtable

Four divorced persons, all believers, talk about pain, recovery, and options

*One thing I do: forgetting what is behind
and straining toward what is ahead,
I press on toward the goal to win the prize
for which God has called me heavenward
in Christ Jesus.*
—Philippians 4:13-14

We convene the meeting, and then we stay out of the way as much as possible.

The members of our roundtable are meeting at a large suburban church for a couple of hours, sipping coffee and munching on cookies left over from the weekend's services. Before we plunge into our discussion let's briefly introduce the four persons who will be sharing their thoughts with you. We've disguised their names: That way, each one feels free to express feelings truly, accurately, and safely—no one will be "quoted" later in a way that might prove embarrassing.

Here are the four members of our divorce roundtable:

- *Elli, age 28, married for three years and divorced for two.* She tells us she is dating someone "fairly seriously" but has not decided about remarriage. "I'm not in a hurry," is how she describes her thoughts about a new union. She is the mother of a four-year-old son.

- *Chris, a man of 47, married twice and divorced twice.* He leads a recovery program for alcoholics and describes himself as a "dry alcoholic." Presently he's not dating anyone; he recently ended a ten-month friendship that did not seem suitable to become his third marriage. He has children from both of his previous marriages but does not have custody of either set of kids. Several of his children are grown adults.

- *Brenda, age 56, was married for eight years, divorced for ten, and has been "happily remarried" (her description) for seventeen.* She has helped organize shelters for battered women, and she leads women's Bible studies and other kinds of female-only small groups at her local church. She is the only member of the round-table who is married. She has children from both marriages. Those from the first marriage are now adults; she has a daughter, age 15, from her current marriage.

- *Jackie, age 35, has been divorced for 18 months after being married for almost six years.* She describes herself as "not ready to even think about getting married again." She has school-age children at home.

Elli, Chris, Brenda, and Jackie will guide us through a wide-ranging discussion of the thoughts, feelings, experiences, and hopes of people who are experiencing divorce and its aftermath.

We open with a simple question: "Would any of you use the term 'healing' or 'healed' from divorce to describe your current reality? Why or why not?"

Chris:

I am healed from my first divorce—mostly healed from my second. But I am "healing" from my own personal brokenness, which was one of many reasons I ended up where I am today—divorced twice. I'm working on a lot of issues that cause me to be the way I am.

Elli:

I'm not sure that "healing" is the way I would look at it. I was afraid, angry, surprised, upset—I was a lot of things when my husband chose to end our marriage. I was an emotional feast: a lot of everything.

Am I "healed" from that? Not really. But time has passed; I have begun to realize again that I'm basically the same person I've always been. I have a little more experience now, and some of that experience isn't pretty. But I'm still a cheerful, hopeful, optimistic person. I'm not sure I need "healing"—I just need more time to pass.

Jackie:

I don't think I've started healing yet, but I need to.

Brenda:

I'm comfortable using the term "healed" about the way I deal with my divorce. In my case, it took three years before I felt normal again. I spent three years in deep anger, a lot of self-hatred—and I had every negative emotion go through me that a person can have.

I didn't hold back, I didn't try to contain it, I expressed my feelings to anyone and everyone. And it took about three years before I started to feel normal. Also, it took a trained counselor seeing me weekly for the third year of that time. But yes, I would say I am healed from my divorce. And it helps a lot to be in a good marriage now, a secure and safe place, with a husband who loves me.

We ask another question: "What's the most difficult thing, or one of the most difficult things, about being a divorced person—especially in the days and months just after the divorce happens?"

Brenda:

You're alone. I mean, you have your kids, and maybe you are blessed to have supportive parents who live nearby. Maybe you have some friends. But the truth is—you are alone. No matter how many people you know, no matter how many friends call you—you are alone.

After you've been married a while, you get used to being "together" and you see your life as "together." All of a sudden, there is no more "together"—there is just you, all by yourself, alone.

It's terrible.

Jackie:

That's exactly where I'm living right now. I have never felt so alone in my entire life. I was single until I was almost 30—but that didn't feel alone. Isn't that weird? But now, after being married—I can't believe it. I am alone, by myself, and I feel isolated, left out, off to the side of everything...

Brenda (hugging Jackie):

Your life is going to get better, and you're going to get better. You've just got to survive this thing for a while. Nothing helps at first—there isn't enough painkiller in the world to take the hurt away.

(The group spends time talking with Jackie and affirming her.)

Chris (returning to the question):

For me, I think the hardest thing about being divorced was feeling like I was a failure. Then when I got divorced a second time, *whoa*—now I was a *total* failure.

I ended up drinking a lot, and some of that was just me feeling like I had wasted my chances, like I had ruined not only my life but my wife's life and my kids' lives. I felt like I had ruined the whole world, kind of single-handedly.

Brenda (to Chris):

How did you get out of that, if you did?

Chris (after thinking for a moment):

Well, I'm not entirely out of it. Part of who I am is...I feel like I've spent a lot of my life failing, letting other people down, not living up to what I could have been. So maybe I'm not out of it yet.

But God has helped me. I'm dry, even though I'm still an alcoholic. And I'm ready to get married again—although it will sure take the right person. I just ended a beautiful relationship with a beautiful person because it just didn't seem like we "fit" in the right way. (He gives a wry grin.) So maybe I'm making progress—now I'm ending the relationship *before* it becomes a marriage, rather than after.

(Everyone laughs, and they need to.)

Elli (returning to the question):

For me, the hardest thing was feeling sorry for my son. I mean, he didn't do anything to deserve losing his parents. Maybe I don't mean "losing them," but you know what I mean. We'll always be his parents, but his family got broken up before he was even three years old!

I looked at him—he could be so cute when he was that age— and I just thought, *Life is so unfair if you have to grow up without your parents.* So I think I focused more on feeling sorry for Jason than I did worrying about myself.

Chris:

I've got two sets of kids that have lost their original parents. Some of my kids are grown now, but they grew up without their real dad. And no matter what I say, or what I do now, I can't make up what they lost.

(The group spends time talking with Chris, listening to him, and sharing their positive views about him as a person, future husband, and father.)

We introduce another question: "What worked, if anything did, to help you start moving forward, start getting better, start making progress?"

Brenda:

Journaling. A friend of mine told me about it just after I got divorced. She had been divorced and seemed confident, even happy, now. So I trusted her opinion about what to try. She told me to just start journaling my thoughts and feelings. She said I shouldn't worry about spelling, or whether I was writing enough, or anything else. She told me to start journaling and to keep doing it.

We insert a quick follow-up question: "How was that helpful to you?"

Brenda:

At first, I'm not sure it was. I'm not a writing kind of person— I hadn't ever kept a journal before. I felt self-conscious and kind of stupid, writing my thoughts down on paper. The only reason I did it is because my friend seemed so confident and sure of herself. So I knew something had worked for her...

How it helped me later was, I would look back at something I wrote a few weeks before, or maybe a few months before. I would remember those feelings. When you journal, it really captures how you feel. I would sit there late at night and read my "old" journal entries, and I would think, *I'm in a different place now than I was then.* I would realize, *Hey, I'm a little better now.*

(We want to note here that recovering from divorce is a long process of getting "a little better now" at your own pace. Keep facing forward and keep moving forward. Time passes, and by the grace of God, you do get "a little better.")

Chris (returning to the question):

I got into a group for divorced dads, guys who didn't see their kids very much. That group led to another group—Al-Anon—which I really needed but hadn't looked for yet. So for me, it was two groups—first a group of guys who were in my same situation, then an AA group that helped me become a dry alcoholic. I'm still close to people in both of those groups. I don't know where I'd be without those people.

Jackie:

I haven't found anything that helps yet, until maybe today. When you all were praying for me a minute ago and talking to me, I just felt so loved and valued. That was maybe the first helpful thing that's happened to me.

(The group reaffirms Jackie, and a useful discussion ensues, all of it related to Jackie's personal and family situation.)

Elli (returning to the question):

For me, it was worship music. I'm not really a writing person—I'm definitely not a group person. And I probably *should* say that what helped me was reading 45 Bible verses a day or something like that. But the truth is, what really helped me was worship music.

I would put on my earphones and listen to my iPod. I would sit there and just let Nichole Nordeman or someone like that sing to me. The lyrics are so real and the songs mean a lot to me. Sometimes I would listen to faster stuff, really upbeat stuff. I like the Katinas, I like Kirk Franklin. For me, when I'm listening to something like that, something that praises God and jumps around a little, it just helps me get out of myself and get into God and whatever's happening.

Brenda:

The music I like is different, but it works the same way. One of the best things I did in my first few years after the divorce was go around the house and start singing praise songs. I'm not a singer—but when I would really get into it and just sing my heart out, I would feel God come and be with me.

Elli:

Exactly. I am closer to God in my music than maybe anywhere else.

Jackie:

I think that might work for me. I haven't been in the mood to listen to happy music. But maybe if I did—it would help. I think you all are convincing me I need to be listening to music—

Brenda:

And singing along with it! Just let it rip. Just sing out loud and don't worry about who hears you. I can tell you—it really works!

(The group spends a few moments talking about contemporary Christian music, comparing notes, and promising to swap CDs and song files.)

We ask what will become our final question: "If you were sitting down today with a newly divorced person and you could only tell them one thing, what one thing would you say to them?"

The group, which has been interactive and lively, sits in silence for a bit, pondering the question. Chris is the first to speak.

Chris:

I'd tell them—work on your issues. Become a better person. No matter what happened to you or whose fault it was, this is the time to work on your own self. Get better. Start making some changes you need to make.

I'm preaching to myself, maybe. But that's what I needed to do. Instead of drowning my sorrows with a bottle of Jack Daniels, I needed to deal with my problem of drinking too much. Instead of blaming myself for being a failure, I needed to find some way to succeed at something.

So I would say: Work on your issues. Get better. Improve yourself.

(There is a pause after Chris speaks, as people reflect on his words.)

Elli:

I would say—anything is possible. When you first get divorced, you start thinking your life has ended, that your future sucks.

But the good news is, that's just not true. Your life has changed, yes, and maybe you're not happy about the changes. Maybe you didn't want your life to change. Maybe you didn't see it coming. Maybe you wish you could stop it.

But your life is changing—and that means anything is possible.

That means a lot of things. For example, maybe you had a pretty good marriage—at least until it started going downhill. Well, guess what? You can have a better marriage the next time, which is partly true because you'll be a better person.

Anything is possible. You can go back to school. You can get a new job. You can start over in brand-new relationships and kind of "invent yourself" all over again. You're not stuck in the same old places, even if they were *good* places—now you are free to start something new.

I would say—anything is possible. Anything!

(Jackie finds hope in this thought. Jackie and Elli converse for a while as everyone else listens.)

Brenda (returning to the question):

I would say, "Hang in there, honey!"

You're going to hurt for a while, probably a long time. You're going to have bad days and worse days. You're going to have absolutely terrible days. You're going to feel more alone, more helpless, more hopeless than you've ever felt in your life. But hang in there!

I was divorced for ten years before I married again. The first three of those years were—by a large margin—the worst three years of my life. Those years were horrible. Almost nothing good was happening—at least not anything I could tell was good, that I could see was happening.

I didn't do anything brilliant—I just hung in there. And little by little, day by day, things got better.

I remember one day when I looked at one of my earlier journal entries that I'd written several months before, and I thought to myself, *I really don't feel that way anymore!* And it was so liberating! I realized that somehow, while I wasn't even paying attention to it, I had gotten better.

So I would say: Hang in there. Just hang in there. Be a survivor, keep getting out of bed in the morning. If you've got kids or someone to take care of—take care of them. Do your best to make them happy and to make them feel safe. Help anybody you can help.

Meanwhile, even if nobody in the world helps you—hang in there.

Jackie:

I don't really have an answer to this question, but I've learned from all three of your answers.

If I could tell a newly divorced person just one thing, I'd say, "Sit down with a group like this! Get around other divorced people, maybe ones that have gotten over it a little bit, and try to learn from them." I've been learning from all of you, this whole time. And this has been exactly what I needed right now.

And I'll tell you another thing. I almost didn't come today. I didn't want to be here. It seemed like a big waste of time. If I wanted to cry, I could stay home and do that. I thought we'd sit around and cry all day.

(The group laughs.)

Jackie (continues):
But instead, this has been the best thing that's happened to me since the divorce. I'm almost starting to feel a little bit hopeful…

Brenda:
So hang in there, honey!

The group laughs again. The laughter is rich with shared experience. There have been tears on these journeys, but today the tears are mixed with some genuine joy. God is good.

Thanks to Our Friends
from the Journey

This book is dedicated to faith-filled people who believed in us very early on our journey—before the process of writing for publication began. These people spoke into our lives both the calling and the blessing of God. They affirmed what God's Spirit was saying within us. Our presence on the pathway is largely a result of knowing some gifted encouragers, including the following five couples.

Dr. Rick and Vicki Power are lifelong friends. All four of us met on the same university campus: Vicki and Lisa shared a common interest in lab work and biology; Rick and David studied philosophy and religion. In the spring of 1978, as university studies came to a close, two marriages occurred in a three-week span: David and Lisa on May 7, Rick and Vicki on May 27.

Rick is a brilliant teacher and deep thinker. Vicki's warm heart opens up in hospitality to all around her. When the two of us despaired of our calling or doubted that doors would ever open for us, Rick and Vicki reminded us of God's presence in our lives and projected optimism and enthusiasm. We came away from coffee or a meal with them—after sharing in seasons of prayer—convinced we should stay the course, keep believing, and wait on the Lord.

Rev. Randy and Lisa Calhoun also kept our dreams alive. They constantly encouraged us to continue with our writing, to keep putting words on paper. Lisa pointed us toward the Christian Writers Guild based in Black Forest, Colorado—an association God used to literally change our lives.

Randy, a TCK (third-culture kid) who grew up on the continent of Africa, is a uniquely gifted children's pastor and ministry director. Lisa, expressing her creative gifts in drama and music at the local church where they serve, has an ongoing counseling ministry to teens. They are accomplished and fruitful writers. They have constantly and consistently reminded us of God's call and God's promises. They have kept us headed in the right directions, staying the course, being faithful. When our own faith or encouragement has lagged, a call from Lisa has restored our hope.

Jeff and Melissa Jakobitz returned from overseas assignments at just the exact moment when we needed godly friends and faithful examples at our sides. As with the two couples mentioned above, we have shared with Jeff and Melissa the joys and accomplishments of our lives—and also the disappointments, setbacks, and deep valleys through which our journey has led.

Jeff's understanding of God's Word and His work, Melissa's passion for the written word and learning—these have steadied us along the way, keeping us focused and obedient in answering the call. Melissa has always assured us that doors would open; Jeff has always reminded us that, as servants, we must keep our focus on faithful obedience rather than any specific outcome.

Rev. Rodger and Sharon Manning have mentored us, prayed for us, and modeled godly marriage and servant leadership in life-changing ways. We have laughed and wept with these close friends through our lives and theirs; we have watched them trust God and honor Him at all times and in all ways.

At an age when some men consider retirement, Rodger is blooming with fresh vision, passionately serving an organization that loves the unreached. Sharon's wisdom and grace have counseled us through the good times and at other times also. Her sharp wit and good humor have encouraged us often.

Finally, *Barry and Pam Stranz* have accepted and loved us while also knowing and seeing our imperfections and immaturities. Barry and Pam joined us in not one but two adventures of a lifetime: a four-week journey by Jeep to the interior of Alaska, camping all the way; and also a somewhat longer journey— planting a community of faith in an urban neighborhood.

Pam is one of Lisa's closest friends and most trusted advisors. In some ways they are two persons with one heart, knowing each other's hopes, dreams, disappointments, and frailties. Barry is a greatly gifted teacher of adults and youth, filled with a vast knowledge of Scripture and human experience. He brings a larger-than-life enthusiasm into any venue in which he serves. As of this writing, God has trusted Barry and Pam with eleven birth children. This is by far the wealthiest couple we know, rich in the treasures that matter most.

In ways we cannot fully understand or explain, our identity is intertwined with the lives of these five couples. We have been shaped and formed by both the intercession and the intervention of these ten caring people. Perhaps not until heaven will we discern their full impact on our journey and its progress.

For all that we have received, we are truly grateful.

Questions for Reflection and Growth

This portion of the book is designed for your personal learning and growth. You can work through the following exercises without reading any of the previous chapters, or you can sit down with them after finishing the book. Either way, this guide is meant for you personally—it is best discovered with a pen or pencil ready, a cup of steaming coffee nearby, and some quiet time set aside for reflection and thought.

As you consider these questions, our prayer is that understanding will begin or continue within your heart and mind. Think of this guide as an early morning: After the dark night of divorce, may the sun rise on new possibilities and fresh discoveries.

As Your Journey Begins

When we wrote this book, our working title was *Facing Forward*. We built the concepts and ideas for this project around the simple idea of looking in the direction you wish to be moving—that is, forward!

As you process your thoughts and feelings about becoming divorced, do you spend more of your time looking backward, thinking about "what might have been" or what you've lost or how unfair everything is? In other words, do you spend a lot of time wrapped up in your personal history?

Or, by contrast, do you spend more of your time thinking about the days ahead, planning for a new life, and dreaming of creative ways to grow, learn, and become?

Although nearly everyone thinks about both their past and their future, most people can identify which of these two possibilities receives most of their attention.

What about you? After thought and reflection, circle the response that most correctly identifies your own journey as of right now.

> **Q:** *Which direction am I facing?*
>
> **A:** *Backward.* I spend a lot of my time thinking about the past, about what has happened to me, about what I've lost, about the pain I've experienced.
>
> **A:** *Forward.* I spend a lot of my time thinking about my future, about new opportunities for me to learn and grow now that I'm suddenly single.

Now let's unpack your answer to this question. Take a moment to list some of the things you see as you face either forward or backward. What you see may be either positive or negative—write down the first things that come to mind and that you realize as you consider the two directions.

When I look backward, here is what I see:

_____

_____

_____

_____

_____

_____

_____

When I look forward, this is what I see:

_____

_____

_____

_____

_____

_____

Now, go back and read through the lists you've made. Would you say most of the items under "looking backward" are positive—or negative? For your list of what you see "looking forward," answer the same question: Are most of the items positive—or negative?

After reviewing your lists, circle an answer for each of the following two statements:

My "backward" list is mostly: POSITIVE   NEGATIVE
My "forward" list is mostly: POSITIVE   NEGATIVE

In general, people recovering from divorce see a lot of pain and damage as they look backward. Although their marriage relationship may have had positive moments and happy experiences, one effect of divorce is to magnify our sense of pain, loss, and suffering. Most divorced people report that their "backward" view is largely—or perhaps entirely—filled with negatives.

For this reason, people recovering from divorce may need practice in looking ahead. When they do look forward, they tend to discover exciting opportunities for growth, learning, and personal development. "Now I can find out who I am," is the way one divorced woman expressed this thought to us at a divorce-recovery seminar we recently led. "It seemed like I spent my whole marriage trying to make my husband happy," she went on, "and guess what? It didn't work. Now maybe I can figure out what makes *me* happy."

While it is true that marriage was never intended to be a situation in which someone's learning and growth are stifled or held back, it is also true that divorce can be a liberating experience, freeing us to discover and identify our own gifts and graces. The simple reality is this: Some of us never learn our purpose in life—never discover our true calling or find our God-given gifts—until divorce happens. Then, even though we weren't seeking it, the shattering of our former life becomes the release of new possibilities.

As Your Journey Continues

Have you ever tried to climb a high mountain—literally? Do you recall the difficulty of trying to breathe the thinner air at a higher altitude? Did you find yourself stopping often along the way, needing times of rest as you trekked upward?

Early in our marriage we bought a Jeep and spent the month of August driving to Alaska. Among other things, we wanted to hike and climb in Denali National Park (formerly called Mt. McKinley National Park). We enjoyed the journey, but we were also focused on the destination.

When we got to Denali, the day was cloudy and overcast. We could not see the peak of Mt. McKinley; in fact, most of the higher mountains were shrouded in mist and fog. We set out anyway, undeterred, all of our pent-up ambitions focused on climbing.

We were trekking on tundra at first. If you've never done this, think about soft, spongy foam rubber. Now imagine a three-feet-deep layer of foam rubber covering a large parking lot, or perhaps a football field. Picture yourself trying to walk from one end of the football field to the other—every step you take, you sink down into three feet of sticky foam. It's almost impossible to keep your balance. It takes a lot of effort to simply pull your feet out of the spongy goo beneath you.

Gradually the tundra gave way to firmer footing. The slopes became steeper and steeper, and we clung close to the side of the mountain. Many times we thought of giving up—when the clouds parted occasionally we could see our tiny little Jeep still parked at the trailhead. How inviting and welcoming it looked way down there, loaded with camping gear, our coolers filled with delicious food!

Setting out for our climb that day, we had realized one thing very quickly: With the difficulty of treading on tundra, the troubles of breathing at higher altitudes, and the sheer physical exertion of a long uphill climb, we needed to travel light. We would have had enough trouble keeping our balance on the narrow trails without trying to juggle the weight of excess baggage! We had quickly changed out of our bulky backpacks, abandoned most of our gear, and scaled down to the mere essentials we needed for survival.

By traveling light, we were now gradually gaining altitude. Our trail was leading us literally through the clouds, upward toward increasingly bright sunlight. With clouds below us, clouds above us, and clouds all around us, often we could see only the rocky trail at our feet. Thankfully, we couldn't always detect the huge drop-offs beside us!

The moment arrived when every mile of our journey, every rain-soaked night of sleeping in our tent, every gallon of overpriced gas suddenly melted into nonexistence. Clinging to the slope of a high mountain, we looked across a wide valley as the clouds parted. Looming over us—it had been there the whole time—was the massive dome of Mt. McKinley, towering over the 14,000-foot peaks around it as if they were zero…nothing.

The sight simply took our breath away: It was a long time before we found our voices and spoke. We were awed into a hush by the sheer magnificence of the unexpected view.

Everything we had suffered was suddenly worth it. Everything we had sacrificed meant nothing at all. The experience of seeing McKinley was priceless.

Just then, as if on cue, an eagle took off from somewhere below us, soaring skyward with outstretched wings. We could not have planned such a moment—it far exceeded the dreams that had propelled us north to Alaska.

Yet we discovered these things by traveling light! We could never have climbed to these heights and seen these breath-taking views if we had tried to carry all our heavy baggage along with us. Lugging our luggage would have kept us far below cloud level. We would have spent our entire vacation down where it was overcast and dark.

Up high, after much effort and suffering, we fed our souls on sweetness and light.

For those who have been divorced, the journey is much the same.

There are unexpected vistas ahead, dramatically beautiful scenes that will take your breath away with amazement and awe. Yet to climb to such heights, you'll need to let go of a lot of your baggage. You'll need to learn how to travel light.

Consider it—what are you holding on to that you need to let go of?

Take a moment to think about the question in terms of your own experience. Think especially about your emotions—are you wrestling with feelings such as jealousy, bitterness, and resentment? Are you struggling under a heavy load of shame or embarrassment over being divorced? Are you burdened with a sense of guilt over somehow not "succeeding" as a married person, feeling as if you are now a failure of some kind?

Emotions such as jealousy, bitterness, and shame are heavy baggage indeed, and they limit our ability to climb new heights of achievement and success.

> **Q:** *What am I holding on to that I need to let go of—so I can reach my highest potential and move forward toward success and new opportunities?*

Here's a list of things that I'm holding on to and need to let go of:

_____

_____

_____

_____

_____

_____

_____

_____

_____

_____

Can you imagine how much lighter you'd feel if you weren't struggling to carry all this baggage around with you? Can you imagine the freedom you'd find without those bulky items strapped on your back? You'd be nimbler, too—able to keep your balance and find your footing on the narrow trails of life.

If you're dreaming of climbing to the high places, you'll need to let go of anything and everything that holds you back and limits your progress. If you want to move up higher, you'll soon discover that the key to gaining altitude is traveling light.

How to Shed Your Emotional Baggage

Among the many negative emotions that cloud the perspective of those of us who end up divorced, there are three that deserve some extra attention and focus. These three responses, all of which are natural and ongoing, can cause us to stagnate, preventing us from being open to needed growth and development. Without noticing it, we can find ourselves locked up and immobilized, trapped where we are, "caught" or "stuck." Here's a look at these three emotions, plus some insight in how to let go of them.

Anger

One of the most normal responses to divorce and abandonment is anger. In fact, if you have experienced a divorce and you're *not* angry, you may need counseling! You may be blocking or denying your true emotions. Normal people get angry when someone breaks promises, abandons commitments, and walks away.

Anger is often a two-part response to unpleasant experiences. The first part of our response centers around something that hurts us, causes pain, or seems unfair. There is an injustice that is happening—something is wrong, and we know it. Yet if we could simply and easily fix what is wrong, we wouldn't get angry. Anger needs a second factor in order to thrive: a sense that we are powerless to change or fix the problem. It is this second factor—our powerlessness in the face of unfair circumstances—that roots anger deeply into our emotional life.

As we noted in an earlier chapter, the billboard on the highway of life tells us the truth: We are not in control. If the world were always fair, if people were always kind and good, it wouldn't matter whether we were in control or not. However, because unfair and unjust things do happen, because pain is caused and suffering indeed happens—and we cannot do anything to change it or fix it—we become angry!

Such anger is normal, natural, and should be expected. However, if we remain angry over a long period of time, we have only ourselves to blame. Before going further, let's stop for a few moments and take a personal inventory:

Q: *What are some of the things I'm angry about in this divorce?*

Now that you've made your list, go back and circle the things that are under your direct control—things you can fix, manage, and change. It's entirely possible, however, that nothing on your list will fit into this category!

As divorce quickly teaches us, there are many things we cannot change or control. So after making a list of some of these things, what options are left for us to consider?

Q: *What can I control about this whole situation I find myself in?*

_____

_____

_____

_____

_____

_____

For most of us, this second list is fairly short. We soon discover that the few things we can control come down to our own words, our own actions, and our own inner feelings or attitudes. Although it may be very difficult for us to keep from speaking out in anger, to refrain from making unhealthy choices, or to transform our innermost thoughts and feelings, here is the truth: *These things are ours to control.*

We may have power over very little else, but our words come from our own lips. Our behavior stems from our own choices. Our feelings happen inside us, not others.

So here is a key strategy to facing our anger and winning a victory over it: We need to change our focus from things we *cannot* control (situations and circumstances, things others say, things others have done to us) to things we *can* learn to control, with God's help. We need to focus on only those few things that are under our own authority and part of our own reality.

Instead of focusing on the impossible, we need to focus on the merely difficult!

The truth is, we can find the help we need to speak more wisely, using helpful words instead of harmful ones. We can get the assistance we need to stop making choices that are unhealthy to ourselves and others. We can even learn, over time, how to "rewire" our thoughts and emotions so we literally feel better as time passes.

None of these things are easy, yet all of them are possible. By contrast, what we cannot do is turn back the clock, put things back the way they were, restore our former dreams to reality. Humpty Dumpty has fallen off the wall—there are too many pieces.

One question may arise: Are we claiming that divorced people can never remarry each other, never find happiness by being restored to their original partner? Of course not. However, even in these rare cases, the remarriage will be a new and different union, not a "going back" to some original time and place. A remarriage of two persons who were previously married will be a journey taken by two new and different people, two people who have been indelibly changed by their experiences, including experiences of brokenness, pain, and new growth. For such a union to survive and succeed, both parties will need to have learned how to focus on things under their own control: their own words, their own actions, their own thoughts and feelings.

This is what the pathway to growth looks like for all of us who experience divorce, including the few who remarry original partners.

Self-Pity

First of all, if we're feeling sorry for ourselves, we have every right to be!

After all, look at what life has dealt us. Look at these lousy cards we have to play. We're expected to win with a hand like this? Better to follow the advice of that country singer: Let's just learn when to "fold 'em."

Here are the some of the things we typically think about when self-pity steals our attention:

- *We look at how difficult our circumstances are.* Life is tough. We don't have the money we need, our kids have "lost" a parent, and we may have been out of the job market for many years. This is difficult!

- *We think no one understands what we're going through.* How could they? They don't know how much we've lost, how hard this has been, how tough it is just to get out of bed every morning and find a reason to get through the day. Who understands the depth of the pain we're in? No one.

- *We may look around our world and wonder, "Why doesn't anyone at least offer to help?"* From our new perspective as divorced people and perhaps single parents, we see others who have seemingly vast financial resources. They're gainfully employed, they own one home or several, their cars are new—they have everything we lack! Why aren't they noticing how poor we are, how much we need? Why aren't they at least making an effort to help the children, for pity's sake? Would that be too much to ask?

In all of these threads of thinking, the common denominator is self-pity. Although we start off with different lines of thought, in the end it comes down to feeling sorry for ourselves that circumstances are so difficult and our situation is so tough. Poor us!

What about you? Did you recognize any of the feelings described here?

Q: *What are some forms of self-pity I am experiencing?*

_____

_____

_____

_____

_____

_____

_____

The path away from self-pity is about this: changing our focus. If we keep on thinking about our own life situation, we'll keep repeating the same negative thoughts we're already experiencing. Therefore, we need to change our focus and think about something else!

Here are some of the pathways other divorced people are discovering. They are ways of focusing outside themselves that are life-changing and health-giving.

First of all, many divorced persons are rediscovering, or finding for the first time, the joy of worship. At a recent divorce-recovery workshop we led in Southern California, we shared the true story of one divorced woman who is attending three worship services every weekend, at three different churches. She finds that the more time she spends centered on God and worship, the less time she spends wrapped up in self-pity.

As we shared this story, a woman in the back row laughed out loud and raised her hand. "I'm doing the same thing!" she exclaimed to the whole group. "I'm going to three different worship services every weekend!" The group laughed and learned at the same time: Here is a constructive substitute for a focus on our own trials and difficulties.

Other divorced persons are finding pathways away from self-pity through music, some as performers and some as listeners. Wrapped up in the sublime experience of music—country gospel, smooth jazz, great hymns of the faith, classic rock—divorced people are discovering ways to change their focus as well as their mood. What some might label "escapism" is in fact a healthy form of getting your attention off yourself. If the lyrics of the music have positive and healthy values—for instance, you're listening to a Christian band—so much the better! You may find yourself praising your way toward better mental health.

Yet another pathway to growth involves looking around at others and finding ways to be helpful. Instead of thinking about how others aren't helping you, change the question to this one: *Who can I help today?* Although you may have few or no financial resources, you can volunteer to do some child care, visit a nursing home or retirement community, or even build homes with Habitat for Humanity. If you start thinking less about yourself and begin to look around at the broader world out there, you'll quickly find others whose situation is even more difficult, more challenging, and more dangerous than your own. Who is lonely today, that you could help with a kind word or a good deed?

Fear

If you're divorced and alone—if you're unemployed, perhaps even homeless—you probably have valid and authentic reasons to be afraid. You're not confused—the simple reality is that difficult and potentially dangerous days lie ahead. Any normal person would be afraid of facing life without a home or a job. Fear is a natural response to these problems!

Yet the problem with fear is that it robs us of our joy. Deeper than "happiness," which is a fleeting emotion at best, joy is something God intends for all of us to possess as our own. Joy is not about our situation or our circumstances. Joy is not about gaining self-esteem because someone seems to find us attractive. Joy is an inward reality that radiates into an outer confidence—at our core, we are filled with God's grace.

Fear, however, robs us of this joy, wrapping us in chains of doubt and despair in several ways:

- *Fear tends to magnify the dangers ahead,* making our problems and difficulties seem even larger than they are. Let's admit the truth: We *are* facing difficult problems! Even so, fear tends to magnify them so they seem extreme. Fear is a lens that distorts problems so they loom over us like giants.

- Meanwhile, *fear tends to minimize our own gifts and strengths.* It causes us to feel week and incapable. We doubt our competence, even if we have functioned through much of our adult life with a reasonable level of maturity, grace, and giftedness. The fear that distorts and magnifies our problems works in reverse on our self-image—it minimizes our own identity and capability. We feel puny and weak.

- Finally, *fear reveals that we are not focusing enough on God.* After all, a God who loves us is certainly larger, wiser, and more powerful than any problem we're afraid of! God helped David defeat Goliath; He helped Gideon's tiny army defeat a much larger fighting force; and He constantly invades human history to defend the weak and support those who face difficult problems. Fear denies God's closeness and His love.

Not surprisingly then, the pathway away from fear begins with a question: "Who's your Daddy?"

If we teach ourselves, if we study the Scripture and learn from the entirety of human experience, we will soon realize our loving heavenly Father delights in coming to the aid of those who need Him most.

God's heart is for the poor—the rich have difficulty getting into heaven.
God's heart is for the weak—the strong are often arrogant and prideful.
God's heart is for the outcast—those ignored by others are God's favorites.

Although fear is entirely natural, it is also normal and rational to turn to an all-powerful God and place our faith in Him. If all others leave us, He will not. When no one else will help us, He will.

In a world of faithlessness and broken promises, we have a Father who has proven Himself over and over again. He is always faithful. He is true and just.

When He says, "I will never leave you or forsake you," that is exactly what He means.

Resources on Divorce and Family Topics

Ministry Organizations and Resources

Association of Marriage and Family Ministries

Primarily a network of speakers, writers, and counselors working in issues related to marriage and family. Website provides links to many helpful resources; this organization also sponsors an annual conference for workers in family ministry.

Web address: www.amfmonline.com

Center for Marriage and Family Studies

Education and encouragement for families in transition; helping families adapt to trauma and change. Primarily tracks in divorce recovery, single parenting, remarriage, and blended families. *Directors:* Dr. David Frisbie and Lisa Frisbie.

Web address: www.MarriageStudies.com

Crown Financial Ministries

Teaching, training, and numerous resources in Christian financial principles, helping families and others manage financial resources according to biblical wisdom and prudent stewardship. *Among founders:* Larry Burkett (d. 2003).

Web address: www.crown.org

Family Life

Speaking, teaching, and special events for couples and families from a Christian perspective, including conferences and seminars. Schedule of upcoming programs and events listed on Web site. *Among principals:* Dennis Rainey.

Web address: www.familylife.com

Focus on the Family

A global ministry organization devoted to strengthening the family through broadcasting, publishing, speaking, and equipping. Produces and publishes numerous resources for many aspects of family life; some materials are available at no cost upon inquiry. Many other resources available for purchase or as gifts with donation to the ongoing ministry. *Founder:* Dr. James Dobson.

Web address: www.family.org

Getting Remarried

A wealth of helpful information related to the preparation and planning of a remarriage, as well as helping remarried couples with all aspects of family life.

Web address: www.gettingremarried.com

Instep Ministries

Programs, resources, and support for single, divorced, and remarried persons from a Christian perspective. Focus on reconciliation, restoration, healing, and hope. *Directors:* Jeff and Judi Parziale.

Web address: www.instepministries.com

Institute for Family Research and Education

Resources and materials for families, including blended families and remarriages. *Directors:* Dr. Donald Partridge and Jenetha Partridge.

Web address: www.ifre.org

Ronald Blue & Company

Christian financial-management services, currently with over 5000 clients and managing over $3 billion in assets. Focus on biblical principles and effective stewardship from a Christian perspective. *Founder:* Ron Blue.

Web address: www.ronblue.com

Smalley Relationship Center

Teaching, speaking, and publishing resources for couples and families. Books, conferences, events at locations nationwide. *Founder:* Dr. Gary Smalley.

Web address: www.dnaofrelationships.com

Stepfamily Association of America

Publishes *Your Stepfamily* magazine. Provides education and support for persons in stepfamilies and for professionals in family therapy. Numerous helpful resources and programs, many with local availability and access.

Web address: www.saafamilies.org

Successful Stepfamilies

Teaching, training, speaking, and publishing materials for stepfamilies providing wisdom from a caring Christian perspective. Conferences at various locations. Numerous helpful links to other related organizations on the Web site. *President:* Ron L. Deal.

Web address: www.SuccessfulStepfamilies.com

Selected Books on Topics Related to Divorce and Families

Adkins, Kay. *I'm Not Your Kid: A Christian's Guide to a Healthy Step-family.* Grand Rapids, Michigan: Baker Books, 2004.

Broersma, Margaret. *Daily Reflections for Stepparents: Living and Loving in a New Family.* Grand Rapids, Michigan: Kregel Publishing, 2003.

Burns, Bob, with Tom Whiteman. *The Fresh Start Divorce Recovery Workbook.* Nashville: Thomas Nelson, 1992.

Chapman, Gary. *Five Signs of a Functional Family.* Chicago: Northfield Publishing, 1997.

Clapp, Genevieve. *Divorce & New Beginnings.* New York: John Wiley & Sons, 2000.

Covey, Stephen R. *First Things First.* New York, Simon and Schuster, 1994.

Croly, Jennifer. *Missing Being Mrs.* Grand Rapids, Michigan: Monarch Books, 2004.

Deal, Ron L. *The Smart Stepfamily: Seven Steps to a Healthy Home.* Minneapolis: Bethany House, 2002.

Frisbie, David and Lisa. *Happily Remarried: Making Decisions Together; Blending Families Successfully; Building a Love That Will Last.* Eugene, Oregon: Harvest House Publishers, 2005.

Gillespie, Natalie Nichols. *The Stepfamily Survival Guide.* Grand Rapids, Michigan: Revell Company, 2004.

Lauer, Robert and Jeanette. *Becoming Family: How to Build a Stepfamily That Really Works.* Minneapolis: Augsburg, 1999.

Omartian, Stormie. *The Power of a Praying Parent.* Eugene, Oregon: Harvest House Publishers, 1995.

Parrott, Les and Leslie. *Saving Your Second Marriage Before It Starts.* Grand Rapids, Michigan: Zondervan, 2001.

Peck, M. Scott. *The Road Less Traveled.* New York: Simon and Schuster, 1978.

Smalley, Gary. *The DNA of Relationships.* Carol Stream, Illinois: Tyndale Publishers, 2004.

Smedes, Lewis B. *Shame and Grace: Healing the Shame We Don't Deserve.* San Francisco: HarperSanFransisco, 1993.

Smoke, Jim. *Growing Through Divorce.* Eugene, Oregon: Harvest House Publishers, 1995.

Virkler, Henry A. *Broken Promises.* Waco, Texas: Word Books, 1992.

Wagonseller, Bill R., with Lynne C. Ruegamer and Marie C. Harrington. *Coping in a Single Parent Home.* New York: Rosen Publishing, 1992.

Wallerstein, Judith S., with Julia M. Lewis and Sandra Blakeslee. *The Unexpected Legacy of Divorce: A 25-Year Landmark Study.* New York: Hyperion, 2000.

Wheat, Ed, and Gloria Oakes Perkins. *Love Life for Every Married Couple.* Grand Rapids, Michigan: Zondervan, 1980.

Counseling, Professional Referrals

National Association of Social Workers

The National Association of Social Workers maintains a network of social service providers in each state, organized through its state chapters. By making contact with the chapter in your state, you can obtain information about providers of counseling and other social services in your city or region.

The NASW Web site maintains a database of information, services, resources, and members which can guide you to locally available providers.

Web address: www.naswdc.org

Information regarding the address and phone number of each state chapter is listed below.

Alabama
2921 Marty Lane #G
Montgomery, AL 36116
(334) 288-2633

Alaska
4220 Resurrection Drive
Anchorage, AK 99504
(907) 332-6279

Arizona
610 W. Broadway #116
Tempe, AZ 85282
(480) 968-4595

Arkansas
1123 S. University, Suite 1010
Little Rock, AR 72204
(501) 663-0658

California
1016 23rd Street
Sacramento, CA 95816
(916) 442-4565

Colorado
6000 E. Evans, Building 1, Suite 121
Denver, CO 80222
(303) 753-8890

Connecticut
2139 Silas Deane Highway,
Suite 205
Rocky Hill, CT 06067
(860) 257-8066

Delaware
3301 Green Street
Claymont, DE 19703
(302) 792-0356

Florida
345 S. Magnolia Drive, Suite 14-B
Tallahassee, FL 32301
(850) 224-2400

Georgia
3070 Presidential Drive, Suite 226
Atlanta, GA 30340
(770) 234-0567

Hawaii
680 Iwilei Road, Suite 665
Honolulu, HI 96817
(808) 521-1787

Idaho
PO Box 7393
Boise, ID 83707
(208) 343-2752

Illinois
180 N. Michigan Avenue,
Suite 400
Chicago, IL 60601
(312) 236-8308

Indiana
1100 W. 42nd Street, Suite 375
Indianapolis, IN 46208
(317) 923-9878

Iowa
4211 Grand Avenue, Level 3
Des Moines, IA 50312
(515) 277-1117

Kansas
Jayhawk Towers
700 S.W. Jackson Street, Suite 801
Topeka, KS 66603-3740

Kentucky
310 St. Clair Street, Suite 104
Frankfort, KY 40601
(270) 223-0245

Louisiana
700 N. 10th Street, Suite 200
Baton Rouge, LA 70802
(225) 346-5035

Maine
222 Water Street
Hallowell, ME 04347
(207) 622-7592

Maryland
5710 Executive Drive
Baltimore, MD 21228
(410) 788-1066

Massachusetts
14 Beacon Street, Suite 409
Boston, MA 02108-3741
(617) 227-9635

Michigan
741 N. Cedar Street, Suite 100
Lansing, MI 48906
(517) 487-1548

Minnesota
1885 W. University Avenue,
Suite 340
St. Paul, MN 55104
(651) 293-1935

Mississippi
PO Box 4228
Jackson, MS 39216
(601) 981-8359

Missouri
Parkade Center, Suite 138
601 Business Loop 70 West
Columbia, MO 65203
(573) 874-6140

Montana
25 S. Ewing, Suite 406
Helena, MT 59601
(406) 449-6208

Nebraska
PO Box 83732
Lincoln, NE 68501
(402) 477-7344

Nevada
1515 E. Flamingo Road, Suite 158
Las Vegas, NV 89119
(702) 791-5872

New Hampshire
c/o New Hampshire Association
of the Blind
25 Walker Street
Concord, NH 03301

New Jersey
2 Quarterbridge Plaza
Hamilton, NJ 08619
(609) 584-5686

New Mexico
1503 University Boulevard N.E.
Albuquerque, NM 87102
(505) 247-2336

New York
New York City Chapter
50 Broadway, 10th Floor
New York, NY 10004
(212) 668-0050

New York State Chapter
188 Washington Avenue
Albany, NY 12210
(518) 463-4741

North Carolina
PO Box 27582
Raleigh, NC 27611-7581
(919) 828-9650

North Dakota
PO Box 1775
Bismarck, ND 58502-1775
(701) 223-4161

Ohio
118 E. Main Street, Suite 3 West
Columbus, OH 43215
(614) 461-4484

Oklahoma
116 East Sheridan, Suite 210
Oklahoma City, OK 73104-2419
(405) 239-7017

Oregon
7688 SW Capitol Highway
Portland, OR 97219
(503) 452-8420

Pennsylvania
1337 N. Front Street
Harrisburg, PA 17102
(717) 758-3588

Rhode Island
260 West Exchange Street
Providence, RI 02903
(401) 274-4940

South Carolina
PO Box 5008
Columbia, SC 29250
(803) 256-8406

South Dakota
1000 N. West Avenue #360
Spearfish, SD 57783
(605) 339-9104

Tennessee
1808 W. End Avenue
Nashville, TN 37203
(615) 321-5095

Texas
810 W. 11th Street
Austin, TX 78701
(512) 474-1454

Utah
University of Utah GSSW,
Room 229
359 S. 1500 East
Salt Lake City, UT 84112-0260
(800) 888-6279

Vermont
PO Box 1348
Montpelier, VT 05601
(802) 223-1713

Virginia
1506 Staples Mill Road
Richmond, VA 23230
(804) 204-1339

Washington
2366 Eastlake Avenue East,
Room 203
Seattle, WA 98102
(206) 322-4344

West Virginia
1608 Virginia Street E.
Charleston, WV 25311
(304) 345-6279

Wisconsin
16 N. Carroll Street, Suite 220
Madison, WI 53703
(608) 257-6334

Wyoming
PO Box 701
Cheyenne, WY 82003
(307) 634-2118

About the Authors

For more than 25 years, Dr. David and Lisa Frisbie have been learning from people who have been divorced. As directors of The Center for Marriage & Family Studies, their study has focused on families in transition—helping families adjust to trauma and change.

The Center for Marriage & Family Studies pursues four primary aspects of learning and growth: divorce recovery, single parenting, postdivorce remarriage, and family life in blended families (stepfamilies). Offering seminars, retreats, workshops, and courses in these four areas, the Center provides effective resources so families in transition can become places of health and wholeness.

David has spoken at retreats, camps, and conferences since 1973. He is the author of several books and numerous articles on topics of marriage and family life, with special emphasis on families that are experiencing change.

David and Lisa have been married for 28 years and make their home in Southern California. Their ministry of encouragement and healing has taken them to each of the 50 United States, 11 of Canada's provinces, and more than two dozen other nations of the world. They have greeted audiences small and large, from many cultures, with words of hope and healing, with good humor, and with topical, up-to-date scholarship.

Media appearances by the Frisbies include those made in *USA Today,* the *New York Times,* and numerous local journals. They have been interviewed on ABC-TV and CBS radio, as well as on many local broadcast stations.

By design, The Center for Marriage & Family Studies is nonpolitical. It neither endorses candidates for elective office nor provides voter guides. It is not affiliated with any church, congregation, or denomination. Neither the Center nor its directors comment on pending legislation or other political issues.

Further information on the Center's programs and activities can be obtained at www.MarriageStudies.com.

- To schedule a presentation or program featuring David or Lisa Frisbie or both, contact:

    Lisa Douglas
    mountainmediagroup@yahoo.com

- To reach David and Lisa Frisbie, please use the following e-mail address:

    Director@MarriageStudies.com

- For information about the Center's resources and programs related to divorce please contact:

    DivorceRecovery@MarriageStudies.com

Happily Remarried

Making Decisions Together • Blending Families Successfully • Building a Love That Will Last

David and Lisa Frisbie

Is Remarriage Right for You?

In North America today, nearly 60 percent of remarriages end in divorce. In *Happily Remarried,* you'll find ways to build the long-term unity that will keep your relationship from becoming just another statistic.

From more than 20 years of speaking, teaching, and counseling, David and Lisa Frisbie understand the situations you face every day. Using many examples drawn from real-life remarriages, they speak with hope and humor about the challenges, leading you through...

- *four key strategies:* forgiving everyone, having a "forever" mind-set, using conflict to get better acquainted, and forming a spiritual connection around God

- *practical marriage-saving advice* on where to live, discipline styles, kids and their feelings, "ex's," and finances

- *questions for discussion and thought* that will help you talk through and think over how the book's advice can apply to *your* circumstances

Combined with the indispensable ingredient of Scripture-based counsel, all of this makes for a great how-to recipe for a successful, happy remarriage!

Includes Helpful Discussion Guide

Read a sample chapter at www.harvesthousepublishers.com

Growing Through Divorce

Jim Smoke

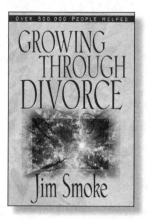

Now that you're here, it's up to you. Go through divorce—or *grow* through divorce!

Shock, adjustment, mourning, and rebuilding. Every person involved in a divorce goes through these stages. Drawing on years of counseling experience, Jim Smoke offers compassion, hope, and practical steps to guide you in your divorce recovery. You'll also discover pitfalls to avoid and how to set attainable growth goals, including...

- looking at the divorce-recovery process as a healing experience
- developing a new support system
- giving yourself the time and permission to experience your emotions
- using your experience to care, share, and support others

Joy and love *can* be yours again. *Growing Through Divorce* shows you how to transform a difficult ending into a fresh beginning.

> *"The book that helped me most cope with the reality of divorce was* Growing Through Divorce... *Powerful...a must-read!"*

Stephen Arterburn
Founder of New Life Ministries and bestselling author

Read a sample chapter at www.harvesthousepublishers.com

From Faking It to Finding Grace

Connie Cavanaugh

Spiritual dryness and disillusionment— nobody ever talks about them. But the truth is, almost every believer experiences periods of dry faith or feeling disconnected from God. Sadly, nearly everyone stays quiet about their doubts, and they feel alone at a time when they need support more than ever.

Writer and speaker Connie Cavanaugh breaks the silence. Because she speaks out of her own ten-year struggle, you can trust her to help lead you toward a deeper and more mature friendship with God. Compassionately, she says,

- "You may feel empty and alienated, but you're not alone in this."
- "Don't try to get back to where you think you once were. Look ahead instead of back."
- "Get ready to listen to the Father, who's never stopped loving you."
- "Hold on to hope—He's calling you back."

"This profoundly relevant and life-changing book will move you, convict you, and encourage and bless you. I urge you to read it."

Richard Blackaby
Coauthor of *Experiencing God Day by Day*

Read a sample chapter at www.harvesthousepublishers.com